Anti-Zionism's
Vitriolic Allegations

To Those Who Support God and <u>His</u> Future Plan for Israel

Anti-Zionism's Vitriolic Allegations

Fred DeRuvo

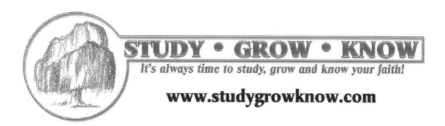

Copyright © 2009 by Study-Grow-Know

All rights reserved. Written permission must be secured from the publisher to use or reproduce any part of this book, except brief quotations in critical reviews or articles.

Published in Scotts Valley, California, by Study-Grow-Know
www.studygrowknow.com • www.adroitpublications.com

Scripture quotations are from The Holy Bible, English Standard Version®, copyright © 2001 by Crossway Bibles, a publishing ministry of Good News Publishers. Used by permission. All rights reserved.

Images used in this publication (unless otherwise noted) are from clipartconnection.com and used with permission, ©2007 JUPITERIMAGES, and its licensors. All rights reserved.

All Woodcuts used herein are in the Public Domain and free of copyright.

All figure illustrations used in this book were created by the author and protected under copyright laws, © 2009.

Cover layout and design: Fred DeRuvo

Library of Congress Cataloging-in-Publication Data

DeRuvo, Fred, 1957 –

ISBN 144217899X
EAN-13 9781442178991

1. Religion – Biblical Theology – Apologetics

Contents

Foreword 6
Before We Begin 7
Chapter 1:   Onward Christian Zionist 13
Chapter 2:   Absolute Ruler 19
Chapter 3:   It's Not All the Same 42
Chapter 4:   Physically Spiritual Jews 58
Chapter 5:   Replacing the Truth 77
Chapter 6:   The Blame Game 102
Chapter 7:   Will Israel Rise Again? 119
Chapter 8:   Cheerleading for God 130
Chapter 9:   Anti-Zionism's Precipice 137
Chapter 10: Ugly Words from Anti-Zionists 160
Chapter 11: Is God Sovereign or Not? 169

ILLUSTRATIONS:
God Creates (Holy) Israel from Root 51
God's Grafting Process 54
The Remnant within Israel and the Church 56
Notes & List of Resources 174

Foreword

Everyone from Covenant Theologians, to Replacement Theologians, to Preterists, believes that God permanently ended His relationship with Israel with the A.D. 70 destruction of Jerusalem and the Temple. They believe they have solid biblical grounds to stand on, which support their conclusions.

Others, like me, believe that God is *not* done with Israel, having plans that remain yet unfulfilled. However, these unfulfilled plans *will* be fulfilled and this will occur in *God's* timing and according to *His* purposes. Those of us who support God and His purposes with Israel are often referred to as Christian Zionists *because* of our support for Israel. In actuality, we support Israel because it appears to us that she remains God's chosen nation.

Too often, those opposed to Christian Zionism express their disapproval with plenty of acrimony and vitriol. This is usually directed to the people who support Israel's right to exist as a sovereign nation.

This book deals with some of the more well known and I believe, false notions propagated by those opposed to Christian Zionism. This book pragmatically refers to these people as *Anti-Zionists*. It is hoped that my efforts here will help *educate*, as well as *eradicate* some of the blatant errors espoused by those who stand in opposition, not only to Israel's right to exist, but ultimately, to God Himself.

- Fred DeRuvo – September 16, 2009

Before We Begin...

Even before human history, Satan attempted to thwart God's purposes. It is of course no surprise then that he would turn his attention to God's favored creation; *man*. Satan was successful in turning both Adam and Eve *away* from God, by tempting them to believe they could become *like* God Himself. His efforts continued after the Garden of Eden, into the time prior to the flood with the introduction of hybrid creatures called Nephilim, and throughout ancient history. In fact, his efforts have never abated.

One of the favored things Satan seems to have focused on is drawing *Israel* away from her God. He has normally attempted this through the enticement of idols, though at times, it was a rebellion in other forms, or by taking God for granted. Satan's goal has been to keep Israel and God *apart*, because Israel, as the *wife of Jehovah*, has a destiny designed by God that it seems fewer and fewer people today are willing to acknowledge, much less support.

In today's day and age, as in history past, Satan has continued working to keep Israel and God separated. He persists in using some within the visible Church to accomplish this age-old goal.

Christian Zionism
Christian Zionism is formed around the idea that the Jewish people (specifically the nation of Israel), continue to be God's chosen people, with unfulfilled prophecies yet to be fulfilled. Because of this, the land that is being fought over in the Middle East - referred to as the Promised Land - **is *still*** God's land.

Christian Zionists support what they believe to be God's plan for a future Israel. We believe that God *again* will one day view the nation of Israel favorably. When this occurs (toward the very end of the seven year Tribulation/Great Tribulation), God will once again save for Himself, the last Remnant of human history, from among Jewish individuals who will be alive at the time. This Remnant will literally go in and possess the land that God promised to Abraham that He would give them until the beginning of the Eternal Order future.

Satan, on the other hand, prefers to have us believe that Israel fell irrevocably out of favor with God with their rejection of Jesus Christ, the Messiah, roughly 2,000 years ago. Certain groups allege that this rejection of Christ was the point at which God ultimately and finally rejected Israel, forever barring any chance of reconciliation. In putting Israel permanently aside, He is then said to have turned His attention to a new entity, the Church. As one of the major tenets of Covenant and Replacement Theological positions (as well as Preterism), this belief has made an indelible mark on church history.

The belief that the Church has now replaced Israel has grown in size and distribution throughout the world over the past few decades. It is this belief that is at odds with God's yet unfulfilled plan for Israel. Unfortunately, those who believe God has, with finality, rejected Israel, regard Christian Zionism as working *against* God.

Some folks are congenial in representing their opinions concerning biblical interpretation. For instance, in an article he wrote, Alan Nairne states, *"[Christians Zionists] usually point out that many of the Church Fathers (i.e. during the first few century ADs) refer to a "millennial kingdom" in which the nation of Israel features prominently. Surely, we may think, they, being so close to the apostolic age should know what the Apostles taught. It is true, where there is clarity of statement (some Fathers are ambiguous), that both views are fairly equally represented. The other view is, of course, that there is no earthly millennial kingdom to follow the Second Coming of Christ. So they are not really any great help. Anyway, we base our view on Scripture, not on the Church Fathers, however valuable their writings may be. All that those Fathers who see a millennial kingdom indicate is that they agree with the views of the Jews, and, perhaps the majority of Jewish Christians of their times. That the Apostles did not so interpret the OT Scriptures I hope to show."*[1]

I would have to agree with Nairne here that the early church fathers were sometimes ambiguous. However, it seems clear that the reason for this has more to do with the fact that, judging from church history, it took centuries for the church to determine its position on Eschatological issues. These issues were not (and are not), as important as the deity of Christ, the doctrine of the Triune God, and salvation by faith alone, which in themselves took a number of centuries to become firmly established.

---

[1] http://www.apocalipsis.org/Israel.htm

Heresy was creeping into the church while Paul was still alive, which is the subject of a number of his epistles. It makes sense that the greater level of energy was expended developing sound doctrinal basics regarding the *fundamentals* of the faith.

Heated Outrage

In spite of charitably worded position statements and/or responses from folks like Alan Nairne, too many individuals are not as charitable. In fact, many are simply downright unpleasant.

Their rejection of Christian Zionism is something more than simple rejection. They actually disallow this view altogether. While it is one thing to vehemently disagree with someone else's theological stance, it is quite another to let loose a barrage of acerbic comments and accusations, all in the name of God. Disagreements over secondary doctrines (or any doctrine really), should *not* be done in a manner, which promotes dissension. All discussion and disagreements should be done with an attitude of love. This is not an easy thing to do at times. It takes restraint, a deliberate desire to glorify God and the strength of His Spirit within to accomplish.

This book is an attempt to respond to the charges put forth by those who are passionately opposed to Christian Zionism. I am hopeful that the demeanor represented here is one in which Christ is fully glorified. Is Christian Zionism satanic? Is it racist? Does it promote unending hurt to Arabs throughout the world? Moreover, is America in danger of being judged by God *because* of Christian Zionism?

It appears that, like anything else in theology where two viewpoints are diametrically opposed, both cannot be true. The task then is to determine which view is the *correct* view. This is accomplished only by going back to God's Word, which is what we shall do throughout this work.

If Christian Zionism is *correct*, and those opposed to it are not, the obvious conclusion is that Satan has been working hard to instill theological error within those camps. These folks believe that the Christian Zionist is *the* reason in which there are so many things wrong in the Middle East, and in America. Because of this thinking, it is important for these individuals to eradicate all support for Israel. Unfortunately, the resulting atmosphere has become very antagonistic.

The most important question that can be asked about this situation is this: *what does God's Word say about it?* What the Bible says about Israel will answer the question, which *should* end the debate. Of course, since the Bible is interpreted in a variety of ways (depending upon which interpretive method is utilized), disagreements often remain.

No theological discussion can take place without considering God's *sovereignty*. His sovereignty is not only part of all He does, but is it obviously the overarching umbrella under which everything that occurs, falls under His watchful eye. The important thing though, is how each person *views* His sovereignty. This will determine how these theological questions are answered.

It is also extremely important to keep in mind the words of Psalm 2. Here we see that God *laughs* at the plans of men. All of our debating changes nothing where God is concerned. While we think we may have reached the answer, if correct, all we are doing is agreeing that God's plan will come to fruition. We are not *making* it happen. God does that, and He needs nothing from us to make it happen.

Flesh and Blood?
Lastly, Paul tells us we are not wrestling against flesh and blood, as so many who are set against Christian Zionism seem to believe. The battle rages in the spiritual realm and it is *there* that it needs to be

fought. Too many within the visible Church are at each other's throats over issues like Israel.

The verbal assaults effused from the Anti-Zionist camp, bring no glory to God. In spite of this, Anti-Zionists believe it is their mission to silence those whom *they* accuse of opposing God.

What needs to be made plain though, for those who have the ability to see, is the *nature* of Christian Zionism, as well as the *nature* of Anti-Zionism. This will become clear once it is understood that God still has plans for the nation of Israel. This, as mentioned, is the crux of the issue. Determining God's purpose will determine which path each Christian must take. We must choose and we must choose wisely, based upon *nothing* more than the correctly interpreted and understood Word of God. It is a challenge, yet it is a challenge that we must not shrink from accepting, because it is evident from the Abrahamic Covenant that God blesses those who bless Israel (from Abraham), and curses those who curse her. This was rescinded when?

Chapter 1
Onward Christian Zionist

The amount of misinformation available today on many subjects related to Christianity is astounding, but not surprising. It makes sense when we consider the fact that Satan, our enemy, is out to try to *undo* whatever God *does*. Satan often attempts to thwart God's work even before God completes it. While he is certainly *not* all knowing, Satan without doubt knows the Bible, *learning* from what God reveals to His children. His attempts to disrupt or destroy God's plans always fall flat of course, but at times, there are a great deal of storm-laden winds and noise surrounding his efforts to destroy God's Church.

From all of this activity, it would be easy to believe that Satan is winning, or at least gaining a foothold, but the truth is that he is absolutely *far from* winning, and will not win. In fact, his *defeat* was clearly manifested at the cross, through Christ's death and resurrection, for the entire universe to witness. Satan's defeat is assured and final. He is, however, *allowed* to do what God permits him to do, until his defeat is made *actual* at a predetermined point in the future.

Satan's Methods
One of the insidious ways Satan works is by creating disunity within the visible Church. This is most frequently accomplished through:

1) *A spiritual illiteracy regarding biblical doctrines,*
2) *An overemphasis on certain aspects of doctrine, or*
3) *The sensationalizing of individual doctrines.*

These three things, coupled with a lack of humility, can easily set Christians against one another. The enemy uses this situation to create compromise, disunity, hatred, and condemnation.

In many cases, the nature of the debate turns into a religious battlefield, complete with name-calling. Results are seen with casualties on both sides. The fallout is often evidenced in arrogance, anger, hatred, lack of forgiveness and pride.

To be clear, there are doctrines that *are* worth fighting for, and the Christian should always be willing and *able* to defend them. Doctrines such as the gospel of Jesus Christ (e.g. salvation by God's grace, through faith in Christ's work on the cross), His deity, the Trinity, the reality of hell, and many other areas of theology should never be given any ground by Christian. Yet, at the same time, it is just as important to know *when* to stop arguing about it. Satan would love nothing more than for those within the visible Church to be in a constant quarrel about some theological subject. If those within the visible Church are consistently embroiled in a religious squabble, they are not *evangelizing*, nor are they *living* for Christ. They are living to *win* the debate.

Recently, in a discussion regarding an aspect of Eschatology, the other person with unconcealed pride, indicated that he had *"never lost a debate!"* He further mentioned a friend of his whom also *"never lost a debate."* When asked who or what the determining factor for deciding the winner was, he had no direct response. It seems clear enough from Scripture that Jesus *never* debated. He *stated*.

Being ready with a biblical response is *mandatory* for every Christian (cf. 1 Peter 3:15). Too many Christians do not know *what* they believe, or *why* they believe it. However, beating someone over the head with a Bible until they "get it" usually accomplishes nothing good (cf. Proverbs 1:22-23). Beyond this, that approach normally creates ill feelings and arrogance.

A Perfect Example
A woman who considers *herself* an authentic Christian, states that Christian Zionists (due to their support for Israel) are:

> *"Fundamentalist Christians" (sometimes called "Fundies") are, characteristically, Zionist, not Christian. In practice, they reject the teaching of Jesus in the New Testament: that each of us is equally precious in the eyes of the Lord. Instead, they live in the world of the Old Testament, where a mean-spirited Jehovah played favorites with his children, giving some (now called "Jews") the OK to commit unspeakable acts of barbarism upon the others ("Gentiles"). Read the Book of Joshua if you don't believe this.*

> *Zionist Fundies will do anything for Israel and "the Jews," whom they worship as God or God's little brother. They are only too happy to be the Jews' slaves, and insist we all join in their bondage. Certainly their beliefs are anti-Christian.*

*More to the point: Zionist "Christians" are **traitors to America**. Along with Jews, they wave the American flag, urging us to spill the blood of any who stand in the way of Israeli ambition. Along with Jews, Zionist Christians scream loudest for Arab blood, even though all rational analysis shouts that Israel and Israeli agents in America were responsible for 9-11. Along with Jews, Zionist Christians would happily have America spill its own blood to help Israel realize its ambitions."*[2] (emphasis added)

The tragedy of Carol A. Valentine's caustic (and untrue) comments quoted above are obvious to anyone who understands that God's completed will for Israel is *yet* to be fulfilled. A number of things become evident immediately upon reading her malicious rhetoric. Apparently, she sees Jehovah as "mean-spirited" based on *her* understanding of the Old Testament (or lack of it), and why God worked the way He worked. Apart from that and the fact that she has made sweeping generalizations, which rest on her opinion only, she has, in one swell swoop, decided that Christian Zionists are:

- *"Fundies" (a negative slur against Fundamentalism)*
- *Not Christian*
- *Those who reject Christ's teaching and authority*
- *Those who do not love all people equally*
- *Unable to understand Scripture (reference to Joshua)*
- *Mean-spirited*
- *Worshippers of Jewish individuals*
- *Willing to be in bondage to Jews*
- *Anti-Christian in their beliefs*
- *Traitors to America*
- *Cheerleaders for Israel's aggressive acts against the Arabs*
- *Warmongers for Israel's cause*

---

[2] http://www.public-action.com/911/chrzion.html

The Common Through Line of Anti-Semitism
The unavoidable conclusion gleaned from her comments, is that Carol A. Valentine is *anti-Semitic*. While she castigates the Christian Zionist for apparently not loving everyone equally, she fails her own test miserably, due to her anti-Semitism! Where is *her* love for Jewish people? This is one of the clearest signs that an individual has misunderstood the Bible and God's purposes, by their view of Israel and Jewish people. Beyond her anti-Semitism, it is also clear that Valentine fails to understand *why* God has chosen to do things the way He has chosen to do them, based on His *sovereign purposes*.

Understandably, no one likes to hear that they may, in fact, be guilty of harboring racist attitudes towards another group. It should also be noted that not all Covenant, Replacement Theologians or Preterists, are anti-Semitic. However, one racist, or anti-Semitic individual is one too many.

While Valentine and others like her are quick to point out what *they* believe to be racism *against* Arabs by those who support Israel, she appears to be completely blind to her own anti-Semitism and the degree to which it exists. Becoming far too common today, this tragedy cannot – *must not* – be overlooked. Anti-Semitism occurs when people do not use the correct hermeneutical approach in their Bible study. This in turn, leads to a faulty interpretation of Scripture.

A common complaint among those who oppose Israel's statehood has to do with the use of our taxes in this country to support Israel. Anti-Zionists are upset over the fact that a large chunk of tax dollars goes to support Israel militarily and financially. Even so, this is not the only place public tax dollars are spent. While the taxes I pay go to support Israel, my taxes are also currently used for many other things with which I do not morally support:

- Abortion
- Subsidizing big business

- Stem cell research, and many other things!

Their Tax Dollars

Anti-Zionists do not like their tax dollars being used to support Israel's "aggression." To them, the fault lies with *Israel* for the conflict, which exists in the Middle East. To support Israel goes against the grain of practical (and they would say, *biblical*) peace. However, in reality, that area of the world has been a continual hotbed of war, corruption, aggression (and all the rest that goes with it), nearly since the beginning of time.

Valentine expresses her sentiments with spite, anger, contempt, and indignation. Though she insists, "*that each of us is equally precious in the eyes of the Lord*," it would appear that this *preciousness* she speaks of, does not extend to those who support Israel, or for that matter, to the Jewish people either. Valentine's view of God's preciousness is myopic, extended primarily to Arab individuals, or those who *support* them.

What we learn from people with beliefs like Valentine's, is that words and motives are directly related to unacknowledged a*nti-Semitism.* This would no doubt be denied, but the Valentine's own words make her position unequivocally clear.

Warfare in the Spiritual Realm

Paul clearly points out that we are not wrestling against flesh and blood, but against powers, and principalities (cf. Ephesians 6:12ff). Anti-Zionists have decided that Paul is wrong, and that we *are,* in fact, wrestling against other people; namely, the Jews.

While condemning Christian Zionism as evil, she remains completely confident in her *own* standing before God. It is clear though, that her words and demeanor call her own Christian testimony into question. Sadly, she seems not in the least concerned.

Chapter 2
Absolute Ruler

To support their position, Anti-Zionists are quick to point to Christ's teachings in the New Testament, while accusing the Christian Zionist of living in the *Old* Testament, and ignoring the teachings of Christ. It seems that those within the Anti-Zionism camp look *only* to Christ's *direct* teachings, largely ignoring Paul and other writers of the New Testament epistles. God's numerous promises *to* Israel, recorded in the Old Testament are also ignored, or simply explained away.

With respect to the Old Testament, some Anti-Zionists have a unique outlook. They point out that Christ Himself came to fulfill the Law (OT). Since He fulfilled it, then *all* of it has been fulfilled, and nothing further is required of the Christian.

In order to clearly understand God's purposes for Israel in the Old Testament, one of the most important rules to observe is the rule of *context*. Context is used daily in all forms of communication. The context largely provides meaning to the thoughts that are written or voiced. If all words had only *one* meaning each, context would not be so important for obvious reasons. Since that is *not* the case however, context becomes an extremely important tool in the interpretative process, in order to gain a correct understanding of Scripture.

Referring again to Alan Nairne's article, he comments on the interpretive process as it relates to salvation;

> *"Salvation-history is continuous from the first promise of redemption given to Adam and Eve following the sin which they brought into the human race. This promise decreed warfare, which would take place between the seed of the serpent and the seed of the woman who would crush the head of the serpent (Gen.3:15). Whilst this warfare would in each generation be played out on the stage of human history, the prophecy related primarily to THE SEED, who is Jesus, the Son of God. Paul makes this clear in the Galatian epistle (3:16) that although Abraham received covenant promises concerning his seed, the promise was not to Abraham's "seeds", the many, but to one SEED, who is Christ. Prophecy largely terminates upon HIM. It is only in Christ we inherit these redemptive promises. Rev.19:10 is to a similar effect - "...the testimony of Jesus is the spirit of prophecy." As Paul states, "Christ is the end of the law unto righteousness to everyone that believes." Rom.10:4. Even when the church was seen afar off in the OT prophecies (Eph.3:5), its purpose was that "...unto him be glory in the church by Christ Jesus throughout all ages, world without end. Amen" (Eph.3:21). And to the Colossians "...he is the head of the body, the church: ....that in all things he might have the preeminence." (Col.1:18).*

In postulating a millennial kingdom, with Jewish dominance, sacrifices, temple, priesthood, etc., there is a subtle shift of emphasis away from Christ's preeminence, to say nothing of it being in plain contradiction to the messages of Galatians and Hebrews, as I hope we shall see.[3]

De-Emphasizing Jesus?

Unfortunately, Nairne seems to miss the point when He speaks of the Millennial Kingdom. He fails to understand the actual context of the Millennial Kingdom. He sees it as Jewish *dominance* and claims, there is a "subtle shift" *away* from Jesus. How can this be true? Is he forgetting that Jesus Himself is *the Absolute* Ruler during this coming period of time? The Temple, along with the newly redesigned sacrificial system all point to Jesus Christ. The fact that Christ is also Jewish serves only to emphasize this point. Jesus is completely *dominant* during the Millennium Kingdom. As Absolute Ruler of the *entire world*, and stationed in Jerusalem, how is the point of the Millennium *not* displaying Jesus as the dominant theme of this period?

Everything about the Millennial Kingdom points *to* Jesus, not away from Him. Let us consider the facts of the Millennium:

The Jewish Remnant will possess the Land, as God's promises are ultimately fulfilled during this period:

- Jesus will reign worldwide, as Absolute Ruler, from Jerusalem
- As Absolute Ruler, Jesus will
    - Establish absolute justice
    - Rule with a rod of iron because the sin nature is resident in humans who live and are born during this time
- Jesus will eradicate problems immediately as they arise
- Jesus will oversee the Temple and all that takes place within it, including the sacrifices

---

[3] http://www.apocalipsis.org/Israel.htm

- Jesus will immediately quell Satan's last attempt to overthrow Him

In all areas, Jesus is supreme, and He will be *seen* as that. The fact that the Jewish Remnant will actually *possess* the Land, as promised, points to God's *truthfulness*. The fact of the Temple points to the fulfillment of Jesus regarding the Law. The newly redesigned sacrificial system serves to remind people the importance of Jesus' sacrifice. It also provides a way for human beings who are *born* during the Millennial Kingdom to come to understand the entire process involved in the sacrifices, as related to Jesus.

Think about what it will be like for people born *during* that time. Unlike our life, they will *see* Christ. They will *hear* Him. They will *experience* life under His physical reign. We do *not*. While He reigns from His Father's throne now, during the Millennium, He will reign physically from His earthly "father's" (David's) throne, as prophesied centuries ago (cf. 1 Chronicles 22:8-10; 2 Chronicles 7:17-18; Psalm 89:3, 4, 27-37; 132:11-12; Jeremiah 23:5-6; Isaiah 11:1-12).

The people who are born into the world during the Millennium will have absolutely *nothing* to compare it with, and certainly, they will be unable to comprehend what life is like for us *now*. They will see Christ in all His glory, reigning supremely, as no one else ever has or ever will.

Sin committed by those *with* a sin nature during the Millennium, will cause a certain amount of strife between people and nations. However, Christ – who will rule with a rod of iron *because* of the sin nature – will deal with problems immediately as they occur. Though not perfect, the Millennial Kingdom will be the closest thing to perfection, this side of the future Eternal Order, which *will* be perfect.

Nairne also seems to miss the full ramifications of what is taught in both Galatians and Hebrews with respect to the fullness of our salvation experience. In actuality, the full truth of these two epistles is yet *future*, and will not become the fully realized, *actual* experience of all the redeemed until the future Eternal Order, beyond the Millennium.

As long as human beings (even redeemed ones), live on earth, the full breadth of these spiritual realities will not the normal experience of redeemed human beings. While Paul tells us that this is the natural experience of all those who – through death or (future) Rapture – live in the heavenly realm, it does not, nor will not, exist in all its fullness, experientially for those of us who, though redeemed, *remain* in their corrupted human bodies. This is extremely important *and impossible* to under emphasize.

Following the Millennial Kingdom, the final resurrection and Great White Throne judgment will occur, followed by a complete and absolute destruction of this present earth and the heavens, which surround it. Following Christ's guided destruction of the earth and heavens, He will make a completely *new* earth, with new heavens surrounding it. At that point, the full extent of everything that Paul speaks of in Galatians, along with the truths taught in Hebrews, will *become* the norm for *everyone*.

Anti-Zionist Says: No Grace for the Jew or Christian Zionist
While Valentine accuses the Christian Zionist of *rejecting* Christ's teachings, she is herself rejecting the very same teachings. Jesus gave commands to *turn the other cheek, be kind to those who despitefully use you, forgive over and over and then again*, and more beyond, but these seem to be *selectively* followed by Anti-Zionists.

It seems that Valentine finds it necessary to chide individuals whom *she* believes do not fall *under* the grace of Christ. While she *states* that we are all precious to God, there is absolutely no evidence that she accepts that Jews and Christian Zionists come under the banner of God's grace and preciousness.

To try to understand her bitterness, it is necessary to determine what Christian Zionism is at its root. What does it stand for? Is it truly possible to be a Christian *and* a Zionist as well, or are these terms mutually exclusive, from a biblical point of view?

As noted in the *Before We Begin* section, Christian Zionists believe that God created Israel to be a *special* people to Him (cf. Exodus 15:13; Deuteronomy 32:18; Jeremiah 2:21; 1 Samuel 12:22, et al). The nation of Israel was created for a special purpose, and was brought into being to be *His* nation. Israel was meant to be the light of the world, shining the truth of God's Word to the nations around her, ultimately pointing to the Messiah, Jesus Christ.

Unbelief Leads to Divorce
We all know that due to Israel's unbelief, the nation consistently failed in their relationship with God. Israel is depicted as the wife of Jehovah in the Old Testament (*already* married to Jehovah), and was a wife who *always* looked for greener pastures. There are many instances in Scripture where God speaks to Israel, as though already married.

One such example is found in Jeremiah 3:14, which states *"Return, O backsliding children," says the LORD; "**for I am married to you**. I will take you, one from a city and two from a family, and I will bring you to Zion,"* (NKJV; emphasis added).

In the book of Hosea, the prophet is told by God to marry a specific woman. This particular woman eventually becomes a harlot, or prostitute, and God wanted Israel to recognize herself in the symbolism of that narrative.

How Does Temporary Become Permanent?
There were times in the Old Testament in which God *temporarily* rejected Israel because of her unfaithfulness. He set her aside temporarily, often ignoring her for hundreds of years at a time. However,

at no time did God ever set His wife aside permanently. There were a number of captivities by foreign nations who took the people of Israel captive, or slaughtered them, or a mix of both. It was only after a time of renewal through their desire to return to Him, that due to His faithfulness, God saw fit to bring them back from their captivity.

It is extremely important to note, that God *never* once rejected them *with finality and permanence.* It is equally significant to recognize that God has always dealt with Israel as a *corporate* body. While He chose specific individuals throughout Israel's history in the Old Testament, He did so to lead and/or unite the entire nation of Israel, but the consequences of their rejection were always meted out to the nation as a whole.

God Always Deals with Israel as One Nation
The wandering in the wilderness for forty years is a perfect example of how God's judgment fell on Israel as a corporate body. Most of us are familiar with the event recorded in Numbers 13-14 that brought God's judgment on the nation.

Moses had sent the twelve spies into the land and when they returned, they gave their report. Ten of the spies were fearful and unconvinced that God could provide the victory over the people in Canaan. Two of the spies – Joshua and Caleb – knew beyond doubt that God *could* and *would* provide the victory. The people of the nation, however, chose to believe the ten naysayers, not Joshua and Caleb. In fact, there was nearly a riot in which the people called for the death of Moses.

This resulted in God stating to Moses that He wanted to wipe Israel out, which prompted Moses to intercede on Israel's behalf. Because of this, God is said to have *relented*. Nevertheless, let's be clear here. God was *not* going to wipe them out at all. He wanted Moses to act as their intercessor, which would bless *Moses*, as well as the people of Israel. God did *not* change His mind. When we speak of God relenting, the text is relating something in human terms, so that we grasp its meaning.

Even though God "relented," judgment still came, with the entire nation forced to wander in the wilderness for forty years. This was done so that every last man from that particular generation above a certain age would die in the wilderness. They had refused to believe God *could* or *would* give them victory, in spite of the many miracles that He had shown them day in and day out. God had decided He was finished with those particular rebels. Interestingly enough, Paul is really commenting on Jewish individuals who were *like* these rebels in the book of Romans (cf. Romans 9-11). When he refers to spiritual Jews vs. physical Jews, it is the latter he has in mind (he is *not* talking about Gentiles here). The authentic Jew is not only physically Jewish, but is one who is circumcised within, in his heart. In either case, the spiritual Jew is *never* Gentile.

Those who died in the wilderness under God's judgment were circumcised *outwardly*, but not *inwardly*. They were, however, still Jewish by *ethnicity*. While circumcision was an outward sign of the covenant with God, it means nothing without the inward circumcision of the heart, which is even more important to God.

So these circumcised, yet unfaithful Jews, fell in the wilderness. At the end of the book of Numbers, every last individual from that previous generation who had rebelled, died in the desert. God was again ready to see if the nation of Israel was willing to take Him at His Word. This they did, at least for the most part. They went into the land and *began* possessing it, this time under Joshua's leadership.

This narrative is only one example of many showing God's dealings with Israel as a nation, or as one unit. The nation often suffered as a whole due to the actions of one. Conversely, the entire nation is often blessed due to the leadership of one (Moses), and God's work on his behalf. What *one* suffers, all suffer, until either God's forgiveness is provided, or His judgment ends, or both. Then Israel starts over with God once again, having come back into fellowship with Him.

This is the way it was for Israel and this is the way it *is* with Israel now, in their current state of unbelief. Ezekiel prophesied about this current situation; that they would return to the land in unbelief (Ezekiel 20:30-38). This is exactly the situation since 1948.

The Regathering of Jews to Israel: Prophecy or Wannabe?
If the regathering of Jews back to Israel is a fulfillment of what is written in Ezekiel 20 as well as other places in Scripture, it is obviously *God*, who is bringing this about. If that is the case, then the Anti-Zionist is fighting God, and this is most assuredly a losing battle.

The Anti-Zionist crowd needs to repent, or they will suffer the consequences of having pitted themselves *against* God, *against* His plan and *against* His nation. It is that simple.

There are numerous passages in Scripture, which detail the fact that God will ultimately have His way with Israel. He will purify them and bring them into submission, not only for their spiritual benefit, but ultimately, for the sake of His Name and His glory. Ezekiel 20 is one such passage.

Ezekiel 20:30-38
"As I live, declares the Lord GOD, surely with a mighty hand and an outstretched arm and with wrath poured out I will be king over you. I will bring you out from the peoples and gather you out of the countries where you are scattered, with a mighty hand and an outstretched arm, and with wrath poured out. And I will bring you into the wilderness of the peoples, and there I will enter into judgment with you face to face. As I entered into judgment with your fathers in the wilderness of the land of Egypt, so I will enter into judgment with you, declares the Lord GOD. I will make you pass under the rod, and I will bring you into the bond of the covenant. I will purge out the rebels from among you, and

those who transgress against me. I will bring them out of the land where they sojourn, but they shall not enter the land of Israel. Then you will know that I am the LORD."

This particular passage is spoken *by* the Lord *to* Israel, *through* the prophet Ezekiel. We are blessed to have it recorded for us so that *we know* what God is going to do. In spite of this written record, many continue to misunderstand and misinterpret what God is saying with respect to Israel.

In short, God is telling Israel that He *will* be their King, whether they like it or not, and He *will* make sure that they *like* it when He has finished with them. Anyone among the Israelites, who does not like it, will be purged out. This is not a pleasant picture because we see that the Lord is basically saying the following things to His wayward wife:

- *He will bend their will to His and will be King over Israel*
- *He will gather them from where they have been scattered*
- *Again He mentions that wrath will be poured out on Israel*
- *He will take them aside and deal with them face to face*
- *He reminds Israel about the judgment He entered into with their forefathers in the wilderness*
- *He will force Israel to pass under the rod[4]*
- *God will enforce His covenant with Israel*
- *He will eradicate any rebellious Jew among the nation*
- *The rebels will not be allowed into the Land of Israel*
- *Because of all this, Israel will know beyond doubt that God is the LORD*

---

[4] "Passing under the rod" is a figure of speech, which is indicative of those times when kings would conquer a nation. They would force the leaders, rulers, and diplomats of that conquered nation to literally bend over and pass under a rod that was held about waist high. This was symbolically saying that they were bowing to their new ruler.

In the final analysis, what we learn is that God *will* accomplish what He sets out to accomplish. He is dependent upon no one, and He allows nothing to stand in the way of His sovereign purposes.

Valley of Dry Bones

Sounds like a name for a song, but it isn't. It begins with a grim picture of dry, dead bones in the valley, which are completely lifeless. In verse four of chapter thirty-seven of Ezekiel, the Lord tells Ezekiel to prophecy over the dead bones. Ezekiel does so and witnesses "*a sound, and behold, a rattling, and the bones came together, bone to its bone. And I looked, and behold, there were sinews on them, and flesh had come upon them, and skin had covered them. But there was no breath in them,*" (Ezekiel 37:7b-8).

Ezekiel is told that he should prophecy again. He does so and "*the breath came into them, and they lived and stood on their feet, an exceedingly great army,*" (Ezekiel 37:10).

In the final phase of this event, we read "*Then he said to me, 'Son of man, these bones are the whole house of Israel. Behold, they say, 'Our bones are dried up, and our hope is lost; we are indeed cut off.' Therefore prophesy, and say to them, Thus says the Lord GOD: Behold, I will open your graves and raise you from your graves, O my people. And I will bring you into the land of Israel. And you shall know that I am the LORD, when I open your graves, and raise you from your graves, O my people. And I will put my Spirit within you, and you shall live, and I will place you in your own land. Then you shall know that I am the LORD; I have spoken, and I will do it, declares the LORD,*" (Ezekiel 37:11-14).

Here, clearly what was once *dead* has been given *life*, over a three-stage process. It did not all occur at once. In spite of how people try to mitigate the importance of the three stages of this passage (or wrongly attempt to apply this to the Church), God Himself has stated in the text that the bones "*are the whole house of Israel.*" This is in keeping with the way God has always dealt with Israel, *one* nation.

He has done so by seeing all of Israel as one unit. Remember though, when Israel is eventually completely restored, we are at that point talking about the *Remnant* for that period of time, which receives Christ just as you, and I received Christ for salvation. This will occur toward the end of the Tribulation period.

Thomas Ice comments on these events in Ezekiel, as related to the house of Israel:

> *"Ezekiel 20:33-38 speaks of a regathering, which must take place before the tribulation. The passage speaks of bringing the nation of Israel back 'from the peoples and gather you from the lands where you are scattered, with a mighty hand and with an outstretched arm and with wrath poured out' (Ezek. 20:34). 'With wrath poured out is a descriptive reference to the tribulation. Thus, in order for this to occur in history, Israel must be back in the land before the tribulation. This passage clearly says that it is the Lord, who is bringing them back. The current nation of Israel is in the process of fulfilling this passage.*
>
> *"In a similar vein, two chapters later, Ezekiel receives another revelation about a future regathering of national Israel (Ezek. 22:17-22). This time, the Lord is 'going to gather you into the midst of Jerusalem' (Ezek. 22:19). Like the metallurgist, the Lord will use the fire of the tribulation to purge out the unfaithful. The Lord is going to 'gather you [Israel] and blow on you with the fire of My wrath, and you will be melted in the midst of it' (Ezek. 22:21). Once again, 'My wrath' depicts the time of the tribulation. It also follows here that the nation must be regathered before that event can take place. The outcome of this event will be that the nation 'will know that I, the Lord, have poured out My wrath on you' (Ezek. 22:22). For this to occur, there must be a regathering by the Lord of Israel to the land, just like we see happening with the modern state of Israel. God is at work through the current state of Israel.*

"Surely, anyone who claims to believe in a national future for Israel would have to say that the valley of dry bones prophecy in some way, shape, or form relates to modern Israel (Ezek.37:1-14). The prophet describes a future process through which the nation of Israel will come to be reconstituted and (when the process is complete), enter a faithful spiritual relationship with the Lord. This multi stage process must surely include the current nation of Israel, in unbelief, that is being prepared to go through a time that will lead to her conversion to Jesus as their Messiah. This is said by Ezekiel to be a work of the Lord (Ezek. 37:14). Thus, the modern state of Israel is a work of God and biblically significant."[5]

Various Interpretations

Generally, the Covenant or Replacement Theologian has this to say about the interpretation related to the Valley of Dry Bones in Ezekiel: *"Ezekiel's vision **probably** does not describe a real valley of dry bones, nor does it **probably** correspond to any real valley with which Ezekiel or his contemporaries were familiar. The ancient Hebrew practice was not to leave dead bodies exposed to the elements, but rather to bury them. There is also no historical record of such a valley. Finally, many of the things that Ezekiel saw in his other visions were not depictions of actual things in the world.*

*The text itself **does not seem** to indicate that Ezekiel was appalled by this vision, but then again, it does not relate every important feature of his reception of the vision. Rather, it relates primarily those details that are important to its interpretation. Certainly, reading the vivid description of the valley and the regeneration of the bodies is somewhat odd, perhaps even appalling, in some sense. Even so, the **ultimate point of the passage is not just to horrify us with gruesome details, but to***

---

[5] http://www.pre-trib.org/article-view.php?id=40

give us hope in the new life that God brings to these dead bones."⁶ (emphasis added)

Allegorizing Away the Truth

As seen, the Covenant/Replacement Theologian simply allegorizes the Scripture into a different meaning, in which that meaning is truncated into a very pedestrian generalization. In the last portion that I have bolded, notice that the person who penned that response simply believes that all people who are lost, but eventually become Christians, are *represented* by the dead bones and God brings life to those who become His through faith in Christ. This is although the text specifically states that God tells Ezekiel that the bones *represent the whole house of Israel*. This is simply changing God's Words to mean something that they did not originally mean. This is done by removing the text from its context.

In order for the Covenant/Replacement Theologian to acknowledge that the bones represent the whole house of Israel *today*, it would have to be admitted that this event witnessed by Ezekiel is *yet* to occur with Israel. History shows that there has never been a time when God has ever resurrected the nation of Israel from a completely dead state prior to 1948, when Israel became a sovereign nation once again. This is then the obvious beginning of the fulfillment of this passage in Ezekiel.

The theologian who stands opposed to a literal interpretation of Scripture is forced to allegorize the passage so that it fits the presuppositions brought to bear on Scripture. It is believed that God fully, finally and completely rejected Israel when the nation's leaders rejected the Messiah. Because this belief by Anti-Zionists is firm, it is natural for them to conclude that Israel's future as a nation contains nothing. As far as God is concerned, He is only dealing with the Church. He has no more dealings with the nation of Israel.

---

[6] http://thirdmill.org/answers/answer.asp/file/99828.qna/category/ot/page/questions/site/iiim

In that sense then, the fact of Israel's statehood has become a major thorn in the flesh to those who set themselves *against* Israel. Their view requires them to view her 1948 statehood as either an accident of nature, or possibly just one more proof of the stubbornness of Jewish people in general. Certainly, it is not believed that God was involved in the 1948 statehood, nor do they believe He is in any way involved with Israel today. It goes without saying, that He will have no involvement with them as a nation in the future either, no matter how the Jews try to find a place for themselves in the Middle East.

This is why those who believe the Church replaced Israel become annoyed and even angered at what is happening in the Middle East today. They see Israel's presence there as a result of their rebellious and stubborn nature, rather than an act of the sovereignty of God. Since the Anti-Zionist believes that Israel is in continued rebellion against *God*, then all "acts of aggression" by Israel simply heap sin upon sin.

Anger Over God's Plans for Israel
Since these theologians interpret Scripture as they do, God seems to have given them over to blindness regarding His plans for Israel. Due to their blindness, they easily become offended and angered when discussing Israel. They have not merely rejected Israel or the Jewish people, but have rejected *God's purposes for* Israel. *That* is a very serious matter to say the least.

This is true of anyone who claims to be a Christian, yet believes and espouses viewpoints, which are inconsistent with the Word of God. Unmasked anger directed toward those who disagree with anti-biblical viewpoint is a telltale sign of Scriptural error.

Another interpretive effort of a group that proclaims they stand for "Salvation of America and the Nation of Israel" has this to say about the Valley of the Dry Bones: *"This story of the dry bones is often mistaken for the re-gathering of Israel that has taken place in our time. The common belief among many is that at the time Israel was established as a nation in 1948 that the fulfillment of the prophecy about the valley of dry bones had come to pass. Many theologians today are agreeing with this belief, that the fulfillment of these scriptures has been taking place since 1948. Most of the people that believe this, likely have good intentions, though have little to no understanding of biblical prophecies concerning Israel. Israel will not be allowed to fully enjoy the Land as an eternal possession until Israel has accepted Jesus Christ as their savior. God himself will not allow it. And this is what the valley of dry bones is all about. It tells of the spiritual rebirth of Israel. The valley of dry bones is a symbolic representation of Israel's spiritual state with God. It is very much like that of any person who is not born again. Before the new birth, the individual is spiritually dead, in trespasses and sins. In the vision of the valley of dry bones, we are told that the bones are very dry (verse 2). This reinforces just how spiritually dead Israel is in this prophecy."*[7]

Regathered in Unbelief by God's Own Hand
Frankly, I am not sure Satan himself could have provided a better interpretation. In studying the above quote, it seems clear that a lack of understanding with respect to the meaning of the vision exists. The individual first states that the Ezekiel passage was *not* fulfilled in 1948, then states that Israel will not possess the land until they receive Jesus Christ as Savior. He does not realize that the resurrection of the dry bones occurs in *stages*, starting with a regathering in *unbelief*.

Scrutiny of this passage reveals that the entire content deals with a *process* over a period time. As we have already indicated, there is a three-part restoration of Israel by God. In the end, the *Remnant* of Israel *will* know Christ as Messiah, Savior, and Lord *before* they go into possess the land after the Great Tribulation. It will be on this basis that they will be *allowed* to enter the land.

---

[7] http://www.americaisraelprophecy.com/drybones.html

The other difficulty with the above interpretation lies in the fact that the passage in Ezekiel is only *one* such passage discussing the regathering of Israel. There are many others, including passages from Jeremiah and Isaiah that support the fact that their regeneration will be a *process* over time. The individual quoted does not realize that from God's own Words, we know that He will be regathering Israel in *wrath,* with an *outstretched arm*. The implication here is that Israel will be regathered, but they will *not* be saved at that time. Their regathering will allow God to literally, deal with their rebellious nature. This will be dealt with *once and for all* during the Tribulation/Great Tribulation, also known as the *time of Jacob's trouble*, or the *time of distress for Jacob* (cf. Jeremiah 30:7).

The Jewish people will return to the Land, thinking *they* are the ones who have decided to return, when in point of fact, it is God, who has caused them to return. The major reason for the Great Tribulation is to *purify* Israel by filtering out the rebels (cf. Ezekiel 20), with only the Remnant *remaining* after the rebels have been purged from Israel.

It is this Remnant to which Paul is referring to in Romans 11:26, which will be saved and will take possession of the Land at the end of the Great Tribulation. The Remnant will fulfill what Christ prophesied in Matthew 23:39 when He specifically stated (to Israel): *"I tell you, you will not see me again, until you say, 'Blessed is he who comes in the name of the Lord."* Look at that chapter. Everything Christ is saying is directed *to* Israel and Israel's religious leaders. The Church is not there. She is not there because the Church does *not* need to be purified, because as Paul clearly explains, this has *already* occurred (Ephesians 1:3;18-19;2:5-6).

Here is the passage from Ezekiel:

"Ezekiel 37: 12: Therefore prophesy and say unto them, Thus saith the Lord GOD; Behold, O my people, I will open your graves, and cause you

to come up out of your graves, and bring you into the land of Israel.
13: And ye shall know that I am the LORD, when I have opened your graves, O my people, and brought you up out of your graves,
*14: And shall **put my spirit in you, and ye shall live**, and **I shall place you in your own land**: then shall ye know that I the LORD have spoken it, and performed it, saith the LORD."*

In spite of the above, the Anti-Zionist states, "*You must realize that this verse is the bottom line for the teaching on the valley of dry bones. It concludes by revealing the mystery of this vision. God was telling Ezekiel that there was a day coming that God would put his spirit in the **hearts of the people of Israel and that they would come alive**. This is exactly what he has done with **every born again believer from the time of the Disciples until today**. His spirit in us is what makes us alive unto God. We are born again.*

There are three things that is [sic] revealed to us in these scriptures:
1. *That Israel will be born again.*
2. *This will happen before Israel is resurrected.*
3. *After they are born again and resurrected from the dead, **God takes them back to the land of Israel**,*"[8] (emphasis added)

Instead of understanding the literal meaning of the text, he allegorizes the text and superimposes it on top of the Church. He agrees that God is speaking to Israel and he agrees that the references *to* Israel are clear. Yet, suddenly, he jumps from Israel to the Church, and he does this – as many do – based on a faulty understanding of Romans 9-11. In that section of Scripture, Paul teaches the difference between a spiritual Jew and one who is merely a physical Jew, as already mentioned. In both cases, the individuals are *Jewish*, not *Gentile*. There is no reference to Gentiles in that specific passage of Romans, as there are none in the Ezekiel passage, which refers specifically to the actual nation of Israel.

---
[8] http://www.americaisraelprophecy.com/drybones.html

The *incorrect assumption* is that the references directed to Israel *now* refer to the Church. It is obvious that God *will* put His Spirit within all people who come to know Him as Savior and Lord. Salvation is exactly the same for Jewish people as well as Gentiles. However, what the quoted person is doing is making the mistake of thinking that God's salvation for *all* is the same as His *will* for all, which is not the case. God's salvation is and has been always the same for Jew and Gentile, but His *will* for them is very different.

God still has a mighty work to perform in Israel. He will do this for the sake of His Name, not for the sake of Israel. The Old Testament is filled with promises made directly *to* the nation of Israel. Many of those promises have not been fulfilled and will *not* be fulfilled in the Church. Because God wants to literally *clear* His Name, He will bring His promises He made to Israel to fruition.

Toward the end of the Great Tribulation, when God's predetermined Jewish Remnant finally realizes their lost condition, they will *earnestly* pray and plead for the return of the Messiah, (Matthew 23:39). In response to their plea, Christ will physically return to *be* their Messiah. The change that will take place within them is exactly what took place within the one thief who hung next to Jesus as their life blood ebbed from both.

The Example of the Thief on the Cross
In Luke 23, we read the short narrative of the thief on the cross. One moment, he was ridiculing, reviling, and blaspheming the Lord, and the next, his eyes were open to the truth of Christ's identity. With this new understanding, he turned to Christ in repentance and simplicity, asking only that he be "remembered" when Christ came into His kingdom. He had obviously gotten to the point of realizing that Christ was, in fact, *the King!* This knowledge underscored his need to repent, and prompted him to plead before this King for the smallest of requests; that he merely be *remembered*.

Christ turned to him, stating just as simply, "*I tell you the truth, today you will be with me in paradise,*" (Luke 23:43). What caused such a drastic change within the heart of the thief? It was the removal of his blinders by the Holy Spirit, which allowed the Truth to penetrate to his soul.

Paul says, in effect, that Israel has been blinded for the sake of the Gentiles, "*Rather through* [Israel's] *trespass* [of rebellion leading to their current blindness] *salvation has come to the Gentiles, so as to make Israel jealous. Now if their trespass means riches for the world, and if their failure means riches for the Gentiles, how much more will their full inclusion mean!*" (Romans 11:11b-12)

As the thief hung dying next to Christ, he was originally blind to our Lord's true nature. However, at one point, his heart was *enlightened* to that truth. There was absolutely *nothing* that this thief could have done to open his own eyes. For reasons known only to God, He chose to bless this man with the knowledge of the Holy, and opened his eyes literally, on his deathbed. Once he saw the truth, it became *his* responsibility to acknowledge and *receive* that truth. This he did, which led to the reward of eternal life.

The Blindness of Today's Jew
As Paul stated, the Jews have been *temporarily* blinded in order for God to extend salvation to the Gentiles, *without* having to go through the nation of Israel first. This is how things were done in the Old Testament (Exodus 13:3), concerning people outside the nation of Israel. Anyone who wanted to worship Israel's God had to become part of that nation, converting *to* Judaism *from* paganism.

Because God hardened Israel's heart *after* their rejection of Jesus, He was then able to reach out directly to Gentiles, bypassing the religious leaders and the nation of Israel completely. The Gentiles would now benefit from Israel's blindness because God now reaches out to the Gentile *directly*. It is Israel's *blindness*, which literally *forwarded to the Gentiles*, the saving grace of Christ through His atonement.

As noted in our Romans 11 quote, Paul speaks of the fact that he wants as many Gentiles as possible to become saved, not only for their sake, but also in order to make the Jewish people jealous; jealous enough to return to God through Jesus Christ!

Anti-Zionist Says: Rejection By God is Final
Anti-Zionists teach that once the leaders of Israel rejected Christ, God's love for Israel waned, growing *permanently* cold. God forever and finally rejected Israel as a nation. These same individuals also tell us that there is *no chance* of God ever *forgiving* or reestablishing ties with the nation of Israel directly. The most that the Jewish people can expect today is individual salvation. The nation of Israel is gone, forever blended *into*, and replaced *by* the Church, which has taken over Israel's favored position and promises.

It is through our union with Christ that Christians (from both Jew and Gentile people groups), are united in Christ as *one* entity. But, the Anti-Zionist tells us that it is also *because* of this union with Christ, that there is no further need for the nation of Israel. Israel as a nation was merely a shadow of the reality now found in Christ.

Since many individuals see Christian Zionism as an affront to God's grace and love, it is viewed as evil, needing to be stamped out. Nevertheless, this view provides no excusable reason for the vitriol and vehemence with which these individuals verbally assault Christian Zionists. They describe Christian Zionists as the modern day Pharisees.

An article written by Charles E. Carlson titled, *Kulchur Klash 2002: Part 1, states the following:*

> *"Many of these self-professed Christian leaders are the Pharisees of today, achieving fame and influence by pleasing the media secular Zionist media powers.*
>
> *"Pharisees were once exclusively Judean, "Jews" in the vernacular of our day. Many contend that Israeli Patriots assert more control over America's political parties, news media and the banking system than is healthy for a Christian society. This should be obvious to anyone who will look at the media; then read the Bible references to Pharisaism. But it is largely from within that the vitality of Christianity is being diluted, not from outside. The control of media may be a "Jewish" problem, but the perversion of Christianity is not. Many professing Christians at all levels of leadership have abandoned their Bible given responsibility in exchange for the footnotes written by men. These are the Pharisees of today."*

In the above quote, Carlson condemns those he says have abandoned their Bible, preferring instead the explanatory notes written by men. He is referring to the study notes written by people like Scofield and those who have followed suit. Note how Carlson barely masks his rancor, which seems to ooze from the very words themselves. Note also how he places quotes around the word *Jews* and *Jewish*, as if merely writing the words fills him with disdain.

Since Carlson equates Christian Zionists with the Pharisees, this removes all vestiges of civility from dealing with the Christian Zionist. In so doing, verbal assaults are accepted in dealing with Christian Zionism and its adherents. Taking their cue from Christ Himself who continually upbraided the religious leaders of His day (mainly Pharisees), the Pharisee *should* be attacked. Who does not think of the Pharisee as someone to resolutely *dislike*, due, mainly to their blind legalism? However, the Christian Zionist is anything *but* blind, or legalistic.

Christ had nothing good thing to say about the Pharisees, did He? For that matter, He said nothing good about the Sadducees or the Scribes either. He went head to head with these groups time after time, repeatedly calling their bluff. He continued His denouncement of them until it was His scheduled time to go to the cross, and then gave Himself to that aspect of the Father's will, as He had given Himself to all other aspects of the Father's will. While the Pharisees planned to kill Christ many times, they were thwarted by God's sovereignty, because it was not His time.

Chapter 3
Not All the Same

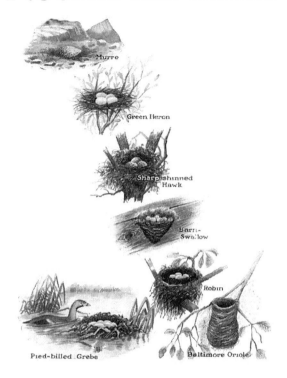

The Wife of Jehovah and the Bride of Christ refer to *two* distinct groups of people, 1) Israel, the wife of Jehovah, and 2) the Church, the Bride of Christ. The situation in the Old Testament regarding Israel is one in which Jehovah is clearly *already* married to her.

There are many occasions in which God says He will give a writ of divorce, which proves that His marriage to Israel existed. As mentioned, the book of Hosea highlights the fact that God *did* divorce Israel. Yet, He did not leave her in that position. He was always wooing her back to Him (cf. Hosea 2:16, 19-20; Isaiah 54:5-8, etc.). It is unthinkable to believe that God would permanently divorce the very people He had created as a special and peculiar people to Himself! This is the Anti-Zionist position.

Regarding the Church, it is nowhere stated that the Church is *currently* married to Jesus. The fact is, this marriage is yet future. The marriage feast, the ceremony; all of it will occur in a future time after Christ's Bride has been received to Him. It is completely incorrect to interchange these two phrases – *the wife of Jehovah* and *the Bride of Christ* – as *if* they refer to the same set of people, because they do *not*.

The Wife of Jehovah has *always* been associated with Jehovah and the Bride of Christ has *always* been connected to Jesus. Since Jehovah and Christ are two different Persons within the Godhead, it is not only incorrect to mix them, but it is unbiblical to do so. It is from this practice of using these terms synonymously that the Anti-Zionist position perpetuates itself today.

Supporting Israel
At its root, Christian Zionism takes the position of supporting Israel because it is God's chosen nation. In the opinion of the Christian Zionist, Israel has *not* ceased to be the chosen nation. They are merely set aside *temporarily* by God until the fullness of the Gentiles comes in, as Paul noted in Romans 9-11.

Christian Zionists are ultimately supporting God, and His purposes. These purposes in support of Israel include the Land that is currently being fought over in the Middle East. Throughout the Bible, the Land is described as *His* Land. Jerusalem is described as *His* city. Israel is described as *His* nation.

One particular website *supporting* Christian Zionism says: *"Christian Zionism seeks to declare the truth of God's word that bequeaths to the people of Israel the Land of Canaan as an everlasting possession. This promise was made by God to Abraham some four thousand years ago (Genesis 13:14-18). Moreover, the promise was reiterated time and* *time again and stressed that loss of domicile, because of rebellion and disobedience, **would not mean loss of possession** (Deuteronomy 30:1-6). The God who exiled the Jewish People on two occasions -586 B.C. and 70 A.D.- has always promised to bring them back and restore their fortunes (Jeremiah 31:10 and Isaiah 11:11). All this because of His promise to Abraham.*[9] (emphasis added)

At its core, that is what Christian Zionism believes. The same website continues with *"From time to time Christian Zionists have been upbraided for leaning too heavily upon the Old Testament for verification of their stand and belief. However, the biblical foundation of Christian Zionism is also found in the New Testament.*[10] This is the clear teaching of Scripture regarding the future scattering of the Jewish people (cf. Luke 21).

Jesus also clearly stated the *regathering* of Israel would occur way into the future, and He described the events surrounding that regathering. It becomes obvious after a careful reading of specific portions of Scripture that God has *not* fully and finally rejected the nation of Israel. To *not* understand this gives rise to erroneous theology. God's plan *does* include regathering *His* people back to *His* land.

Christian Zionism is defined in many ways. Some of the definitions are more correct than others. Paul Richard Wilkinson says that Christian Zionism *"properly defined, incorporates the following key elements:*

1. *A clear, Biblical distinction between Israel and the Church.*
2. *The any moment, pre-tribulation Rapture of the Church.*
3. *The return of the Jews to the Land.*
4. *The rebuilding of the Temple.*
5. *The rise of the Antichrist.*
6. *A seven-year period known as the Great Tribulation.*

---

[9] http://christianactionforisrael.org/4thcongress2.html
[10] Ibid

7. *The national salvation of the Jews.*
8. *The return of Christ to Jerusalem.*
9. *The thousand-year reign of Christ on earth.*"[11]

One of the major keys that should be kept continually in mind is that the Christian Zionist sees a unique plan for Israel and a separate unique plan for the Church. This does *not* mean that God has two modes of *salvation*; one for Israel and one for the Church. This is not the case at all. Just as God's will for one individual is quite different from His will for the next, God's will for Israel is different from His will for the Church.

The line of demarcation between the Church and Israel has become extremely blurred by those who see no unique plan in God's purposes for the future state of Israel. Since it is too often stated that Israel has actually been replaced by the Church, it is commonplace in today's church-going society to hear Christians refer to themselves as "spiritual Jews" or "real Jews", though they are *Gentile* Christians. These Christians unfortunately misunderstand Paul's simple and clear teachings in Romans where he discusses what it means to be a true Jew.

In the context of those passages, Paul is not referring *to* Gentiles. He is dealing specifically with Jewish individuals at that point in his epistle to the Romans. He is making a distinction between a true Jew and a false Jew, but *both* are Jews. This is important to grasp because it sets the stage for what he eventually says about the nation of Israel later in Romans.

Paul's Words and Teachings

In looking at the book of Romans then, we must understand that Paul begins in chapter one by explaining that no one is free from guilt and all are under judgment; the Jew, the Gentile, the pagan etc. Paul then

---

[11] Paul Richard Wilkinson *For Zion's Sake* (Colorado Springs: Paternoster 2007), 13-14

discusses each ethnicity individually so that he cannot be misunderstood.

The clear difference between Christian Zionism and those diametrically opposed to it stems from how one understands Paul's statements in Romans chapters nine through eleven. We all read the same words that Paul wrote, yet we do not all come away with the same meaning.

One author makes a number of erroneous statements about the real identity of the seed of Abraham as well as what constitutes a real Jew. It will be helpful to look at how this individual interprets Paul's words, and we can then compare that to Scripture to determine if they are correct or not.

Who is the True Jew?

"Paul's definition of who is an heir of Abraham and who is not, [is] revealed primarily in the third and fourth chapters of Galatians and the ninth through eleventh chapters of Romans."[12] This same individual – Theodore Winston Pike – continues by first looking at Romans chapter nine. *"St. Paul drops a theological bombshell. He states that not everyone who is born of Jewish parents and educated in the synagogue is a Jew. 'For they are not all Israel which are Israel: Neither, because they are the seed of Abraham, are they all children: but, In Isaac shall they seed be called. That is, they which are the children of the flesh, these are not the children of God: but the children of the promise are counted for the seed' (Romans 9:6-8)."*[13]

Immediately after this statement, Pike announces, *"Good orthodox Jews of pure descent are 'not the seed of Abraham'? Can the earth bear such words? Did not Paul realize that the Christian church today stands trembling before the Jew because it believes him to be the "seed of Abraham," inheritor of his ancient patriarchal privileges, and that*

---

[12] Theodore Winston Pike, *Israel Our Duty...Our Dilemma* (Big Sky Press 2003), 8
[13] Ibid, 8

the nation of Israel lays claim to Palestine because such was promised to the "seed of Abraham"?"[14]

Unfortunately, Pike already has it terribly wrong. Notice that he is not only convinced that he has it *correct*, but his foray into sarcasm underscores that point. Pike maintains, "*Good orthodox Jews of pure descent are 'not the seed of Abraham'* which is presented as a sweeping generalization. This statement implies that **no** Jewish person is really the true seed of Abraham. This is a complete misunderstanding of Paul's words. This type of mistake is extremely easy to make if the *context* is ignored. Paul makes no such comment. He is not *eliminating* Jewish individuals at all.

If we consider the biblical text of Romans closely, Paul is actually saying that just because someone *comes from Abraham's seed,* it does not make them a true, *spiritual* Jew, no more than being part of Israel in the Old Testament made someone part of the Remnant. Put another way, Paul affirms that only those Jewish people who are "born again," are those he calls "spiritual Jews" from Abraham's seed. These individuals *believe* God and, are saved because of it, just as Abraham was and just as Gentiles are saved.

However, let us continue with Pike's statement, and attempt to follow his line of thinking. He asks who makes up the actual Remnant? "*Paul tells us the true 'seed' of Abraham constitutes a pure remnant in every age, which has been chosen by God for salvation.*"[15]

So far, so good. This is exactly what Paul is saying. Just because someone is a Jew, it does mean that they are part of the Remnant. Just so that we are clear though, one must ask exactly *where* did God keep that Remnant? It was always hidden *within* the nation of Israel, *never* outside of Israel, within other nations. **This is Paul's teaching in Romans 9-11.**

---

[14] Ibid, 9
[15] Theodore Winston Pike, *Israel Our Duty...Our Dilemma* (Big Sky Press 2003), 9

Pike continues, "*Hebrew Christians constituted the descendants of a 'remnant' within Israel, which had always existed in its center, despite the apostasy surrounding.*"[16] This is good, and Pike continues to be right on track here.

Pike then states, "*Paul continues to equate the New Testament church with this remnant, repeating God's answer to Elijah after his victory over the prophets of Baal on Mt. Carmel…in Romans 11:7, St. Paul describes this Christian* **Remnant as those who had really grasped the meaning of Israel.** *Israel of the flesh did not comprehend their Messiah – only Israel of the spirit, for the rest were blinded.*"[17] (emphasis added)

Whoops!! He was doing *so well*, until he made this huge jump by moving completely *away* from Israel to the Church. Yet, it is clear from the earlier text in Romans chapter nine, that Paul only had *Jewish individuals* in mind, *not* Gentiles, as has been repeatedly pointed out. Therefore, he *cannot* be referring to the Church. In fact, though he points out in chapter nine of Romans that salvation is for *both* the Jew and the Gentiles, Paul goes right back to the Remnant of Israel by quoting Isaiah, "*Though the number of the sons of Israel be as the sand of the sea, only a remnant of them will be saved,*" (Romans 9:27).

I have heard it said that the reference to Israel "as the sand of the sea" could not possibly be simply referring *only* to Jewish individuals. Therefore, Isaiah must have included Christian Gentiles too. This is going way beyond the meaning of the text. It is clear from the OT alone that the Israelites, upon exiting Egypt could have had numbers totaling six hundred three thousand five hundred fifty, (cf. Numbers 1:46). If that was the original number of people *leaving* Egypt at the beginning of their travels, it should not be difficult to believe that

---

[16] Ibid, 10
[17] Ibid, 10

their numbers would grow so large that they would become *like* the sand of sea.

However, it *is* also possible that God *was* referencing the total number of people who would become heirs to *salvation* that came from and through Abraham's seed; Jesus Christ. This is certainly possible. Even this though, does not negate the other promises that God made to Abraham. In fact, if this is what God meant, then it confirms that the other promises made to Abraham were *just* as valid.

In the quote above, Pike makes the grand mistake of taking Paul's words like "my brethren," "my kinsman," or "my people," to mean *Gentiles*, when in point of fact, the *entire context* is referencing Jewish individuals. This makes sense given that Paul *himself* while a Christian, remained *Jewish*. Being Jewish concerns *ethnicity*, and does not change even after becoming a believer. In fact, while on earth, *no person's* ethnicity or gender changes after becoming a Christian.

Alan Nairne goes so far as to say that "*We must conclude from these Scriptures that the olive tree of Romans chapter eleven is nothing less than the totality of the promises to Abraham.*"[18] However, this conclusion is hardly logical, given the fact that Paul has been comparing *unregenerate* Jewish people with *regenerate* Jewish people. The *only* promise that is extended to everyone regardless of ethnicity, nationality, or gender is that of *salvation* through the Redeemer, Jesus Christ.

In chapter eleven of Romans, Paul is clearly referring to Jews *from* Israel. He also refers to how Elijah felt believing he was the *only* person who stood for God, yet it turned out not to be the case. Paul says *"I ask, then, has God rejected his people? By no means! For I myself am an Israelite, a descendant of Abraham, a member of the tribe of Benjamin. God has not rejected his people whom he foreknew. Do you not*

---

[18] http://www.apocalipsis.org/Israel.htm

know what the Scripture says of Elijah, how he appeals to God against Israel? "Lord, they have killed your prophets, they have demolished your altars, and I alone am left, and they seek my life." But what is God's reply to him? "I have kept for myself seven thousand men who have not bowed the knee to Baal." So too at the present time there is a remnant, chosen by grace. But if it is by grace, it is no longer on the basis of works; otherwise grace would no longer be grace," Romans 11:1-6.

Nairne, Pike, and others seem unable to reconcile the fact that this Remnant that God spoke of with Elijah came *directly from* within Israel. Pike believes that Paul is referring to some "Christian" Remnant (whatever that is) referencing, *"In Romans 11:7, St. Paul describes this Christian remnant as those who had really grasped the meaning of Israel. Israel of the flesh did not comprehend their Messiah – only Israel of the spirit, for the rest were blinded."* In spite of what Pike believes, this is an obvious reference to the state of Israel as a nation and the Remnant *within* Israel.

Dr. Arnold G. Fruchtenbaum comments on the Romans passage just quoted. He states, *"The point of verses 1-10 then, is that while Israel as a nation has failed to attain righteousness, this rejection of the Messiahship of Jesus is not a total rejection; there are Jewish people who do believe. These Jewish believers have attained the righteousness of God. At the present time, there are Jewish believers that are the Remnant according to the election of grace. So instead of using the existence of a minority of believers as evidence that God has cast off His people, in reality, it is evidence that He has not."*

So it should be clear that the Remnant is *not* made up of both Jewish people and Gentile people. The Remnant includes those Jewish people *from* the nation of Israel. If we understand Paul to be stating this, then the entire Olive Tree scenario becomes plainly clear.

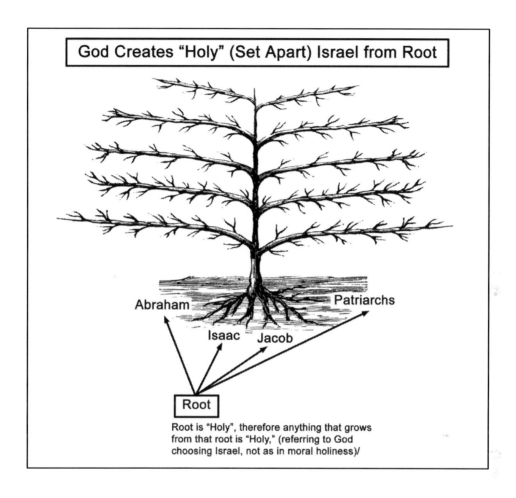

Paul's point, according to Dr. Fruchtenbaum (and one in which this author is in agreement), is that God has vouchsafed His Remnant by placing it *alongside* the Church (during this current period of history), but the entirety of the Church is *not* the Remnant. Do you see the difference? In actuality, the Church is *attached* to the Remnant.

Dr. Fruchtenbaum continues, *"The point Paul makes is that it was God's plan for Israel to reject the Messiahship of Jesus; for a while, [so that] the gospel would go out to the Gentiles, during which time they were to provoke Jews to jealousy; until eventually, all Israel is saved. Paul builds upon Isaiah 49:1-13, where Isaiah taught the same thing: that the Messiah would come to Israel, Israel would reject Him, and the*

Messiah would then, for a while, become the light to the Gentiles; but eventually, Israel [as a nation <u>from</u> the Remnant] will return to Him and be restored."[19]

To misinterpret Paul's clear teaching leads directly to the error that the Church has permanently replaced Israel. This belief is arrived at only by *erroneously* interpreting the passages here in Romans and elsewhere.

A careful reading of the entire book of Romans, with special emphasis on chapters nine through eleven, reveals that this belief about the Church replacing Israel is a completely *unbiblical* notion, yet people continue to believe and espouse it. It is an untenable position arrived at by either ignoring or misconstruing the context. In spite of this, Anti-Zionists state that *their* belief is the correct one and the Christian Zionist suffers from a case of seriously misinterpreting Scripture.

So how do we determine which belief is the correct belief? Like anything else, it can only be accomplished through the careful exegesis of God's Word. His Word must be studied in all its fullness, allowing Scripture to interpret Scripture, in order to arrive at the correct conclusion. Sifting through the complexities of Scripture can be difficult because of the many contexts that need to be considered in order to arrive at proper conclusions. We have begun to do this, but let's take the time to look even more closely at the Olive Tree and what God's Word states.

The Olive Tree
Paul continues his argument in Romans 11, by using the example of an Olive Tree:

"So I ask, did they stumble in order that they might fall? By no means! Rather through their trespass salvation has come to the Gentiles, so as

---
[19] Ibid, 783

to make Israel jealous. Now if their trespass means riches for the world, and if their failure means riches for the Gentiles, how much more will their full inclusion mean!

Now I am speaking to you Gentiles. Inasmuch then as I am an apostle to the Gentiles, I magnify my ministry in order somehow to make my fellow Jews jealous, and thus save some of them. For if their rejection means the reconciliation of the world, what will their acceptance mean but life from the dead? If the dough offered as firstfruits is holy, so is the whole lump, and if the root is holy, so are the branches.

But if some of the branches were broken off, and you, although a wild olive shoot, were grafted in among the others and now share in the nourishing root of the olive tree, do not be arrogant toward the branches. If you are, remember it is not you who support the root, but the root that supports you. Then you will say, "Branches were broken off so that I might be grafted in." That is true. They were broken off because of their unbelief, but you stand fast through faith. So do not become proud, but fear. For if God did not spare the natural branches, neither will he spare you. Note then the kindness and the severity of God: severity toward those who have fallen, but God's kindness to you, provided you continue in his kindness. Otherwise you too will be cut off. And even they, if they do not continue in their unbelief, will be grafted in, for God has the power to graft them in again. For if you were cut from what is by nature a wild olive tree, and grafted, contrary to nature, into a cultivated olive tree, how much more will these, the natural branches, be grafted back into their own olive tree," (Romans 11:11-24).

The main point of Paul's teaching regarding the Olive Tree is that it represents as Dr. Fruchtenbaum and other commentators refer to as the *place of blessing*. It does *not* represent an individual's salvation.

Just as some of the natural Jewish branches were pruned off and wild olive Gentile branches grafted in, God can just as easily reverse the

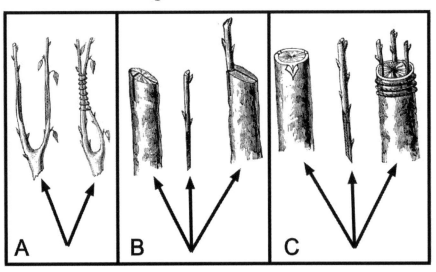

God's Grafting Process for the Church

There are many ways to graft foreign branches into a tree or vine, as shown by the illustrations A, B, and C. What **never** changes though is that the foreign branch that is grafted in, **never** establishes its identity as the original tree. The foreign branch always remains what it was originally created to be, but now, having been grafted into another tree, receives the nutrients and strength that it was unable to obtain by itself.

If not for this tree that the foreign branch was grafted into, it would have **died**, but now, because it has been grafted into **another** source that is teaming with life, this foreign branch now thrives. This is the Church. The Church has been grafted into the tree which is not only owned by another (Israel), but we are foreigners to it. In spite of this though, we are blessed to receive from this tree what we would not otherwise be able to obtain without it.

situation. This is why Paul is so careful to insist that the Gentiles should not boast in any way at all about the fact that some Jewish branches have been removed to make room for Gentile branches. It is *God* who does the pruning and grafting, and it is *He* who receives the praise and glory. This cannot refer to *salvation*, as salvation is something that is eternally guaranteed by God, with the Holy Spirit's seal acting as a guarantee. Salvation *cannot* be removed as pruning removes branches.

The Olive Tree's *lump* and *natural branches* also represent Israel (cf. Romans 11:16). The actual *root* of the tree goes all the way back to Abraham, Isaac, Jacob, and the Abrahamic Covenant itself, and that root gave birth to Israel.

Fruchtenbaum states *"The Olive Tree in this passage does* **not** *represent Israel or the Church; it represents the place of spiritual blessing. Israel is the owner of the Olive Tree, but Israel is not the tree itself. The root of this place of blessing is the Abrahamic Covenant. Paul makes the same point here that he made in Ephesians 2:11-16 and 3:5-6...The Gentiles are not 'takers-over' but 'partakers of Jewish spiritual blessings'."*[20]

Gentiles Grafted *Into* the Olive Tree

The entire Olive Tree is of *Jewish* origin! Please note that Gentile Christians are *grafted into the Olive Tree*. It is *not* the other way around. Believing Jews are *not* grafted into anything *Gentile*. This is extremely important to understand. In essence, then, Christian Gentiles are now receiving the *blessings* of salvation *because they have been grafted into* the Olive Tree owned by Israel. The Olive Tree always remains Jewish in heritage. Gentiles are privileged to *share* in the *salvific* blessings (of the Abrahamic Covenant), by their connection to the Olive Tree through the grafting process.

Gentiles have *no* claim to the root, the lump, the dough, or anything else connected to that tree. Gentile branches are the *wild* branches that essentially do not belong to that tree. God's grace, however, has caused the Gentiles, who place their faith in Him, to benefit from their association *with* the Olive Tree. This *still* does not mean that Gentile Christians are *spiritual Jews*, no more than an orphaned kitten being nursed by a dog, along with her *own* litter of puppies *becomes* a "spiritual" dog.

---

[20] Arnold G. Fruchtenbaum, *Footsteps of the Messiah* (San Antonio: Ariel Ministries), 784

Israel and the Remnant Within

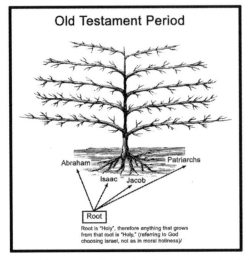

God has ALWAYS dealt with Israel as ONE nation. Once created, His Remnant was kept INSIDE the nation of Israel. ALL Jews - physical and spiritual - are considered Israelites, but only the **spiritual** Jews are ever part of the TRUE Israel (the Remnant).

Remnant of Israel and the Church

Once God created the Church (kept secret from the Prophets), He continued with His Remnant, with the Church being established as each new believer is grafted into the same Olive Tree as the Remnant. Once the fullness of Gentiles comes in, God will **Rapture** the Church and once again deal with unregenerate Israel.

Toward the end of his book, Pike arrives at an untenable, yet not surprising conclusion. Without equivocation he states that Israel has *no biblical* right to occupy Palestine. This is one of the main doctrines of the Replacement Theologian's belief. He arrives there because of his faulty interpretation with respect to Paul's arguments in Romans and Galatians.

Chapter 4
Physically Spiritual Jews

Theodore Pike uses Galatians as proof of Paul teaching that the type of person who truly constitutes an authentic (or spiritual) Jew, is not based on ethnicity. If you are familiar with Galatians, you know that Paul was dealing with the fact that the believers in the churches throughout Galatia, were being deceived into thinking that salvation was *not* of grace alone, but was instead by grace *plus* works. In this case, it was the work of *circumcision*.

Paul goes through the painstaking process of pointing out to the Galatian believers that works of the flesh did *nothing* to save anyone, ever. In fact, he clarifies for them, that all who live under the Law are also under a *curse* (cf. Galatians 3:10). This is because it is impossible for man to uphold every aspect of the Law. Jesus – being fully God and fully Man – was the only One to accomplish this, and of course, the blessing of salvation comes to us *because* of *His* ability to keep the Law. Salvation creates sanctification, which lasts our lifetime.

However, we need to be certain we understand the *context* in which this letter was written by the apostle. Alan Nairne, commenting on Galatians, states, "*The NT makes it quite clear that the nation, land, priesthood, tabernacle, temple, offerings, were, like Eden, and so much else, picture books of the reality that was to come, and a vehicle to ensure that God's Deliverer would be able to come in the 'fullness of time'. What kind of duration was envisaged for the law - and, by implication the nation? 'Until the seed should come to whom the promises were made' (Gal.3:19).*"[21]

Nairne states that all things, which foreshadowed Christ, are fulfilled in Him. These "picture books" are merely the shadow of the reality found in Christ. Why though, is Nairne including *all* the promises given to Abraham, while Paul is only dealing with *salvation* in the book of Galatians? There is most certainly an *eternal* reality found within the Abrahamic Covenant. Because of that, it is safe to say that this reality exists within *eternity*, not in our current dimension of *time*. The only people, who are *currently* experiencing the full and complete reality of the priesthood, tabernacle, etc., are those believers who have died and entered into that *eternal* existence, where Christ is physically seen and experienced.

By including the nation, the land, the priesthood, the tabernacle, and the rest, as he has done, Nairne *wrongly* assumes that by referring to the Law in Galatians 3, Paul must be referring to *all aspects* of the Abrahamic Covenant. However, this is neither a *realistic*, nor *an accurate* assumption.

---

[21] http://www.apocalipsis.org/Israel.htm

The Law given to Israel through Moses, was not intended to supplant (or even fulfill) all aspects of the Abrahamic Covenant. It was to do two things: 1) *point to the reality that the Law could not bring about salvation,* and *2) point to the forthcoming eternal salvation, which would be available through the Messiah.* While the Law pointed out the *fact of sin*, it also, by implication, pointed out the *need for a Savior.* Again though, it is all related to the doctrine of *salvation*, which Paul is covering in Galatians. This is why Paul brings it up in the first place, because of the danger that existed for the Galatian churches. They were being deceived into thinking that going *back* to the Law was what provided salvation. The Judaizers, who were attempting to deceive the new believers in the churches of the Galatian province, were effectively stating that these *converts* to Christianity must *also* follow the laws of Judaism, *including* the covenant of circumcision. *Then*, these new believers were free to be Christians.

The problem of course is that the Judaizers had no faith in Christ's expiation. Like many cults today – whether Jehovah's Witnesses, Mormons, or something else – their faith is in some type of *work* that they believe must be accomplished in order to obtain salvation.

Paul states, *"Why then was the law given? It was added because of transgressions, until the arrival of the descendant to whom the promise had been made,"* (Galatians 3:19 NET). Regarding the same passage, Nairne states, *"Concerning the covenant at Sinai, we need to understand that, in essence, nothing had changed. Paul tells us (Gal.3:19) that the law was added, or, came alongside, that which was already in existence - i.e. the Abrahamic promises. That is, the Abrahamic covenant "embraced" the Mosaic covenant. The way of personal salvation, revealed in the Garden of Eden, (Gen.3:21; 4:4) through faith and sacrifice, was still the same for each individual. The "Law" was given, not to procure salvation, but to provide a format within which godly Hebrews could, as a matter of love to their God, in thankfulness, and in the spirit of the law (see Deut.10:16 & 30:6) live lives that were pleasing to him."*

While on one hand, Nairne seems to understand that the part of the Abrahamic Covenant Paul is dealing with in Galatians, is that which pertains to *salvation*, Nairne unfortunately believes that salvation for *Gentiles* fulfills or includes *all aspects* of the Abrahamic Covenant. However, this is not true.

Concerning the letter to the Galatians, we know that this letter was written circa A.D. 49. We also know that the book of Acts covers a period of roughly thirty years, so this letter was written about seventeen years into the book of Acts, making the church fairly young at this point. During this time, the majority of the Church was largely made up of Jewish believers and this is a very important fact, which needs to be considered and brought into the equation.

We learn from the book of Acts, as Paul went through the various provinces of Asia, and other parts of the known world, that he *always* went to the Jews first. Normally, after presenting the Jewish people with the gospel message in their synagogues, some would hear and receive his message, becoming converted in the process. It was *because of this conversion of Jewish people,* that certain orthodox Jewish men followed Paul from place to place. They attempted to *undo* what Paul did, and tried to keep him from spreading the message of Christ to *other* Jewish people. When the Jewish leaders would eventually reject Paul because of the message he brought, he would at that point go to the Gentiles, presenting the same message of salvation, where it was usually more eagerly received.

Paul: "I Persecuted the Church"

Paul speaks of persecuting the church in the opening verses of Galatians, chapter one (vv. 13-14), as part of his *former* life. He speaks of his zeal on behalf of Judaism. He understands *why* there are certain individuals who are literally sneaking in, for the purposes of ensuring that these converts to Christianity (both Jew and Gentile), obeyed the Laws of Judaism, since Christianity was originally seen as being a small sect within the nation of Israel (Galatians 1:6-10). Though they think they are trying to *correct* wayward Jews and Gentile proselytes to Judaism, they are really *perverting* the gospel of Jesus Christ.

Paul also spends a good portion of Galatians chapters one and two proving the authenticity of his apostleship. Why did he take the time to do this? Because it is obvious that the Judaizers attempted to cast doubt on Paul's credentials. They sought to *undermine* his ministry and his authority. If they could successfully accomplish this, they would have the upper hand in gaining the favor of the Jewish and Gentile believers in the churches of Galatia.

The entire issue at stake in the letter to the Galatians can be summed up in one word: *salvation*! Paul speaks a great deal on this subject throughout Galatians. He is constantly comparing and contrasting the Law given through Moses, with the freedom purchased through Christ.

Circumcision is the covenant sign between the Jewish people of Israel and God. To Judaizers, it was this particular sign that meant the difference between receiving salvation and not receiving it. Without circumcision, they believed it was impossible to have God's salvation, because He was not approachable without it.

In 2:16ff, Paul states, "*We ourselves are Jews by birth and not Gentile sinners; yet we know that a person is not justified by works of the law but through faith in Jesus Christ,*" Gal 2:15-16 (ESV).

Notice that Paul says "we," indicating that he is including himself as he talks with people who were also Jewish, in these churches. Paul also *differentiates* between Jews and Gentiles, even though he soon speaks of the fact that all differences between men and women, slave and free, Jew and Gentile have been eradicated. Is Paul contradicting himself? Please read on.

We know from Acts 13 and following, that wherever Paul went to preach the gospel, he went to the synagogues first. He was normally heard, at least initially, until some Jewish individuals decided he was preaching heresy. Though a number of Jewish people received the gospel, it was *because* of this that he was normally chased out of town, or worse. He would *then* take his message of the gospel to the Gentiles.

In chapter three, Paul states, *"Know then that it is those of faith who are the sons of Abraham. And the Scripture, foreseeing that God would justify the Gentiles by faith, preached the gospel beforehand to Abraham, saying, 'In you shall all the nations be blessed.' So then, those who are of faith are blessed along with Abraham, the man of faith. Gal 3:7-9 (ESV)."* Please note that Paul is speaking *about* Jews here, whom he calls *"the sons of Abraham"* (*those of faith*). He *then* speaks about Gentiles, pointing out that the gospel would be *extended* to them as well. Later in this same chapter, Paul teaches that the Abrahamic Covenant is still being upheld *through* Christ, not negated.

In chapter three, beginning with verse 28, Paul states, *"There is neither Jew nor Greek, there is neither slave nor free, there is no male and female, for you are all one in Christ Jesus. And if you are Christ's, then you are Abraham's offspring, heirs according to promise,"* Gal 3:28-29 (ESV).

What does *"heirs according to promise"* mean? We know that the entirety of Galatians is dealing with the subject of *salvation*. Paul is dealing with *no other* aspect of the Abrahamic Covenant. He is dealing *only* with *salvation*, and does so by comparing the Law with Grace; slave with free. Salvation is now extended *through* Christ to all nations and all people. Israel has been *temporarily* set aside (as we learn in Romans 9-11), in order for this to occur.

The Issue Involves the Word "Temporary"
If Israel was set aside **temporarily**, there must be an *end* to this *setting aside*, because the very word "*temporarily"* implies an ending. If God has set Israel aside for a while, we must ask, *from what* is God

setting them aside? There must be something He is *not* doing with them, though He is obviously *still* saving individual Jewish people. Paul is proof of that, as well as Barnabas, and others.

What is God *not* doing with Israel now, that He was doing *before* they rejected Christ? There are only two things that God is *not* doing with the Jewish people *now*:

1. *He is not now currently working with Israel as a nation.*
2. *He is not now currently fulfilling all remaining aspects of the Abrahamic Covenant (aside from salvation for all).*

These are the only logical conclusions that can be arrived at, while maintaining the integrity of Scripture. God must have obviously placed aspects of the Abrahamic Covenant *on hold,* and if they are on hold temporarily, then at some point in time, God will *lift* this temporary hold, to once again deal with Israel as a nation. Do we have any idea *when* this temporary hold that God has placed on Israel will expire? Yes, we do and it is also in Romans 9-11, which we will get to shortly.

If God had *not* set Israel aside, He would be required to extend the gospel message to the Gentiles *through* the nation of Israel, as He did in the Old Testament. Since the nation of Israel rejected Christ, God rejected Israel, but as stated, *only temporarily.*

Returning to Galatians 5, we note that Paul is *still* speaking about *circumcision.* Even toward the end of chapter six, Paul *continues* speaking about circumcision. When he closes with the phrase "the Israel of God," he is speaking about the *Jewish* Remnant, which comes from *within* the nation of Israel. During his day, Paul was *part* of God's Remnant of Israel - the Israel of God - for that generation.

What of the Distinctions?
Theodore Pike understands the Galatians 3:28-29 passage to be a text proving that all ethnic and gender distinctions have been erased,

now. Alan Nairne believes the same thing, stating, *"Paul writing to both the Ephesian Christians (Eph.2:11-22) and those at Colossae (3:10-11) makes it clear that racial and national distinctions are forever gone."*[22]

Paul does state this is the case, but what does he *mean*? This is where some might say that I should be taking things literally. I plan to do just that, as soon as I know what Paul *means* in this section. When I speak of understanding the Bible in *literal* terms, I am *always* referring to interpreting the Bible so that its literal *meaning* becomes plain. In order to do that, I must know everything I can know about the passage, including the *context*. All of this together, allows me to *literally* understand what Paul is actually *stating*.

Most commentators believe that Paul wrote Galatians before he wrote any other book. If this is so, then why does Paul take pains to tell Timothy later, that there *are* rules for men and women in church (cf. 1 Timothy 2:12-13)? 1 Timothy came *after* Galatians. Beyond this, Paul (and Peter) spends a good amount of time discussing the *roles* in marriage (cf. Ephesians 5:21-25; Colossians 3:18-19; 1 Peter 3:1-7). How could this be, if Paul was *in reality* teaching that all ethnic and gender distinctions are gone *now*, in this life? Again, is Paul contradicting himself here? No, there is no contradiction.

It should be obvious that Paul is referring to the fact that *in Christ* – meaning in the *spiritual* realm (cf. 3:26) – we are *one* without distinction, because we *are* already the perfected Bride of Christ in the spiritual realm. Essentially, in eternity at the marriage of the Lamb, all within the Church will represent the *one* Bride. At that point, it is obvious that all gender, racial and positional distinctions are *gone*. In fact, in the spiritual realm, they *are* gone now. However, in *this* temporal realm, they still exist.

---

[22] http://www.apocalipsis.org/Israel.htm

If these distinctions were non-existent *now*, the following would be true:

- Same sex marriage would be fine.
- Women pastors would be fine.
- Paul would have condemned slavery during his day.
- There would have been no reason to issue qualifications of bishop, elder, pastor, deacon, or deaconess.
- No specific male-female roles would exist in marriage.
- Paul would not have honored Israel by stating that Gentiles owe a debt to Jews, since salvation comes from them (cf. Romans 9-11).
- Paul would not have continued offering the gospel to the Jews first, and *then* the Gentiles on his missionary journeys.

In reality, this does not happen as long as the Bride of Christ remains on this earth. No Christian is perfect in this life. We will *never* reach a state of sinless perfection while we live here, in our flesh. It will only be when we see our Savior in person, that we will be *like* Him (cf. 1 John 3:2). Beyond this of course, while the Bride of Christ is *one* in Him, some members of the Bride are currently and actually *with* Him, while others are here on earth, and there are some who have not yet been born.

Paul is *not* teaching that *here on earth*, all distinctions are *erased*. If that is what he was saying, then he *would* obviously be contradicting himself later, in other books. He cannot be stating that here on earth, in our imperfect vessels of clay, all distinctions have been set aside *now*. While all are equal now, *roles* exist.

The Differences are IN Christ
Since the entire letter to the Galatian churches deals with *salvation*, which is a spiritual work, it should be apparent that Paul is teaching that as far as *salvation* is concerned, there is *no* difference between people. It does not matter if someone is a *king*, or a *slave*, a *man* or a

woman, a *Jewish* individual or a *Gentile* person. In each case, *all* people have the very same ability to receive salvation from the hand of Christ, and *without distinction*. Beyond this, once salvation is received, it instantly grants *equality* between all those who share in that salvation. There is no difference between a man and a woman as far as the spiritual benefits of salvation are concerned. There is no distinction with those who are slaves in this life and those who are not. Because of Christ, and the spiritual significance of His salvation, there is not one difference between Jewish *believers* and Gentile *believers*. All are equal in God's sight. All are equally loved and equally forgiven.

This is what Paul is teaching. Salvation is for *all* people, irrespective of gender, race, or position in life. Paul is *not* teaching that these distinctions are removed while we are here in this life. He *supports* some of these distinctions to the letters to Titus and Timothy. To Philemon, he never stated that he should set Onesimus *free*, because Onesimus was already free in Christ!

Moreover, throughout the book of Acts, even *after* Paul wrote his letter to the Galatian churches, he continued to go to the Jewish synagogues, offering the gospel to the Jews *first*, and *then* to the Gentiles, thereby placing the Jewish person *first* (though not superior to the Gentile). If he was in truth teaching that all distinctions are now gone, these actions on his part would be hypocritical at best, because he would be doing other than what he preached. Paul did not do that.

If Paul had seriously *meant* that all distinctions had been removed during this physical lifetime, he would have preached the gospel to all people regardless of their ethnicity, position or gender, and not have always gone to the Jew *first*. It is clear though that Paul does not view these distinctions as having been removed during this earthly sojourn. He continues to maintain a distinction and a privileged position between Jews and Gentiles.

Paul says something along similar lines in his letter to the Ephesians, written circa late 50s A.D., some ten or so years *after* he composed his letter to the Galatian churches. He makes this statement, "*God, being rich in mercy, because of the great love with which he loved us, even when we were dead in our trespasses, made us alive together with Christ— by grace you have been saved— and raised us up with him and seated us with him in the heavenly places in Christ Jesus*," (Ephesians 2:4-6).

Seated in the Heavenlies?
This is another spiritual truth that must be analyzed in order to know exactly what Paul means. Paul is saying that *right now*, every Christian is seated with Christ in the heavenly realm. This means that in the *spiritual* realm, all Christians are already *with* Christ. We are as good as *there,* because God sees us there already. Paul must be referring to the spiritual realm, because physically, Christians alive now are not in heaven. In fact, it is our aging, dying physical bodies that keep our spirits tied to this earthly realm.

Paul is saying that *because* our spirits are already seated with our Lord Jesus Christ (in Him), we benefit from that as we live the remainder of our lives here, *on earth*. Through the Holy Spirit, our spirits are already seated with Christ. This is part of the guarantee that we *will physically* be with Christ *after* we die. Our lives are now hidden in Christ, *spiritually*. We gain tremendously from that truth.

In spite of this spiritual truth though, my body continues to age and one day, I will die. I might get sick from time to time here on this earth, or I may develop a life-threatening disease, which the Lord may use to call me home. However, our lives are now hidden in Christ, spiritually. This spiritual truth is *significant*.

We also must consider the fact that eternity is outside the realm of our fourth dimension; *time*. In eternity, all things are already completely done. Everything that God established in eternity past has come to fruition. They *are as good as done*, because He established all these things in eternity past, before Creation. Paul alludes to this truth numerous times throughout his letters. What God has previously determined, He *has*, *is*, and *will* bring to pass. Though I may be seated with Christ in the heavenlies *now*, I am certainly *not* enjoying that position to its fullest degree.

How can it be said that all the distinctions are now gone, here in this physical realm, when in point of fact, we do not have the physical, or mental perfection to go along with it? That seems like the exact situation that *would* have existed for Adam and Eve, had they been able to eat of the tree of life, *after* they had sinned.

In this life, no matter how much we allow (through our submission to Him) Christ to live His life in and through us, what remains is the surety of our continued *imperfection* in this life. There is no way that we can enjoy *all the* benefits of being in Christ as our experience *now*, yet we know full well that other benefits, which are more important are *not* ours practically speaking, in the *now*. The sin nature, which gives rise to all forms of self-centeredness and lawlessness, is still the thing that tends to guide my decisions, as sad as that may be.

No matter how much time I spend reading my Bible, praying, endeavoring to walk with Christ, and submitting myself to Him, the truth remains that I will *never* be perfect in this life. It is absurd to walk around emphasizing a lack of distinctions from people to people, when it is quite obvious that distinctions (*not* inequalities; but distinctions), exist now.

I know that God sees me as being fully righteous. To Him, my sin is gone – past, present and future. When I *do* sin in this life, it behooves me to confess it to Him as soon as I realize what has occurred, but I do not need to ask for His forgiveness, because His forgiveness has already been applied to me. It is a fact and foregone conclusion that because of my salvation, all of my individual sins are gone. Even though God sees Christ's righteousness as *mine*, this is not the reality for me in this life. If it was true in a practical measure, that Christ's righteousness was mine, then I would be completely done sinning. I would, in essence, be living in sinless perfection. That would be nice, but it is not the truth for my existence here and now.

It is confusing why some believe that certain things are gone now, while other things remain, yet Paul is always referring to the fact that in the heavenly realms, or in the future, when we see Christ, these things will be perfectly active. However, these things are not perfectly active in us now.

While we are unable to know and experience the full force of the blessing of actually *being with* Christ physically *now*, our spirit benefits greatly. Certainly, aspects of that truth affect our attitude and demeanor, *here* and *now*. Our life here on earth is blessed by our spirit's association with Christ now. We grow, mature, and become more like Christ because of it. However, *after* we die, we will enjoy the *full* benefits of our union with Christ.

Christians Who Have Died
My sister went home to be with the Lord November 2, 2008. She *now* fully experiences Christ's presence. Moreover, she does not sin, nor does she experience sickness. She has no difficulty with weight control, fatigue, hunger, thirst, or any of the things that we experience in this life. Beyond all of this, distinctions are gone for her and all other believers who are now with Christ. This is certainly not my experience though. In fact, as I write this, my stomach is telling me that it is time to stop and take a lunch break. To continue to go without food means fatigue, tiredness and an inability to think properly.

Food provides fuel, feeding my body and brain, in order that I might do the best work I can as I write this. Without food, my body will begin to live off itself and draw blood away from those areas that need it, focusing on the areas that require it more than others because of a lack of food. My brain will have less oxygen, and my thinking will become clouded. My sister does not experience this at all and one day, when I am with her, her current experience will be mine as well.

Paul often referred to things in the spiritual realm that we cannot see and certainly cannot fully appreciate, or fully experience now. Nonetheless, these spiritual blessings and benefits are real, and we profit from them because we are *in* Christ now. When we enter heaven with Christ, the *entire Body,* we call the Church, will at that point be completely united into *one,* with absolutely *no* distinction between ethnicity, position, gender, or even doctrine.

Satan is Now Defeated

It is clear from Scripture that Satan is defeated. This occurred at the cross. When Jesus died, then rose again, He sealed the absolute and final victory over Satan. At the appointed time, Satan will be cast into the Lake of Fire, joining the Antichrist. This is as good as if it has already taken place. Yet, it has *not* actually taken place. Satan still roams the earth, accusing Christians, as Peter points out. Satan seeks his own will and endeavors to overthrow God's will at every turn.

Christians know that Satan *is* defeated and will be defeated practically speaking. We also know that *now,* in this life, as we live prior to the Lord's return, Satan in many ways, can still gain the upper hand over us, as God allows. Who would say though that although Satan *will* be thrown in the Lake of Fire, that it may not happen? It *will* happen because of the victory of the cross. However, we are forced to live with the current fact that Satan exists and is free to wreak havoc (as overseen and allowed by God). Those Christians who have gone on to be with the Lord are now beyond Satan's sphere of influence. He cannot directly affect their existence by tempting them to sin, or causing them to become ill. They are now protected from that because of their spiritual state. We are not, though one day we will also enjoy that perfect existence.

Because Satan is a defeated foe, (of which his end is *sure*), we know that one day, we will be completely free from the maliciousness we endure because of Him. In His defeat, He is still allowed to do what he can to thwart God. In reality, though, far from thwarting God, God uses Satan to complete His purposes.

The truth of the situation is that Satan *is* defeated, in spite of the fact that Christians living today must still be on their guard against him and his schemes. None of his efforts though, takes away from the fact that his defeat came about at Calvary's cross, even though the *carrying* out of his sentence is still *yet* future.

The fact that Paul speaks of a lack of distinctions can ultimately only refer to the eternal state. How can anyone really believe that this is the case *now* as we live within our physical tents here? Paul is *not* teaching that all distinctions are gone now, nor is he teaching that *everything* promised to Abraham's seed has been *fulfilled in the Church.* This is plain because all that he discusses in his letter to the Galatian believers has to do with *salvation*. He does *not* discuss the land, nor does he discuss any other portion of the Abrahamic Covenant.

Anti-Semitism Securely In Place
The Anti-Zionist reacts to the Christian Zionist position of viewing Israel and the Jewish people *favorably*, with anti-Semitism. One of the websites we quoted from earlier says this about anti-Semitism within the Church, "*Unfortunately the Church, being more concerned with her own interests, has failed historically to heed these clear warnings and the result has been arrogance, pride and anti-Semitism. There is a clear link between anti-Semitism and the Church over the centuries of history, and Replacement Theology has made a major contribution to this evil.*"[23]

---

[23] http://christianactionforisrael.org/4thcongress2.html

It is not difficult to see how insidious this form of anti-Semitism has become. In many articles and books, the position is usually espoused that all people should be defended, *except* the Jewish person. The amount of anger, vitriol, and contempt for Jews, as well as those who support them, is readily seen in the results of what these individuals say, write and *advocate*. In spite of all the good that Luther did for instance, with respect to stripping away the additional works that Roman Catholicism had placed upon salvation by grace alone, he was still unfortunately, very anti-Semitic, as some of his writings have shown (cf. *The Jews and Their Lies*).

Returning to Carol A. Valentine, this comment of hers bears further consideration; "*Read the Book of Joshua if you don't believe this.*" Here, she has just finished commenting on the "mean-spirited Jehovah," playing favorites with the nation of Israel and the unspeakable atrocities they committed in His Name. Then she points us to the book of Joshua.

We can assume Valentine is implying that Israel's actions toward those who were already occupying parts of the Promised Land, was blatantly *wrong*. This is in spite of the fact *God* instructed them to go into the Land of Canaan and deal with the people who lived there as *His arm of judgment*. It is clear that Valentine's difficulty lies in the fact that the *Jews* were commanded to rid the land of *Gentiles*. So her point seems to be that the Jews have *always* gone after the Gentiles.

In believing that what the Jews perpetrated against Gentiles was wrong, Valentine apparently considers the actions of the Jewish people to be *racist*. Of necessity she disagrees with Scripture, which states that what Israel did, was done by order of God. This is extremely ironic, since she obviously does not see her own anti-Semitism, yet can point to (alleged) racist tendencies and actions *from* Jew *toward* Gentile.

Kill Them All in Canaan

Whether Valentine or anyone else believes that what Israel did was due to God's commands is beside the point. Scripture indicates that God had some very good reasons to use Israel as His arm of judgment against the nations that lived in the Promised Land. If we look at the text in both Numbers and Joshua, clearly the land had *giants* in it. This same word appears in Genesis 6 where we learn that giants existed in the world in those days. These giants were very powerful individuals, not merely in strength, but in mental ability as well.

It is believed by many commentators that these giants, known as Nephilim, existed as the result of sexual union between *fallen angels* and human women. How that actually took place is not known (and certainly some things are better not known). It seems that the text which says, *"the sons of God saw the daughters of men, that they were beautiful; and they took wives for themselves of all whom they chose,"* (Genesis 6:2) indicates an intermingling.[24]

From this intermingling, a human-hybrid race was the result, which if left unchecked, would eventually corrupt the *entire* human DNA. How then would the Messiah be born?

This mutated offspring was the largest reason why God had to destroy the ancient world, saving only Noah and his family. Apparently, Noah and his family had not had their DNA corrupted by any unions with angelic beings, according to Genesis 6.

When Moses and the children of Israel first arrived at the borders of the Land of Canaan, they saw these giants (cf. Numbers 13; also Deu-

---

[24] The phrase "sons of God" is normally understood as angelic beings for a number of reasons. It is not my purpose to argue for or against the Sethian lineage as being a candidate for "sons of God." There are plenty of books and articles that have already been written on that subject. Suffice it to say that I am satisfied that there was an actual co-mingling between fallen angel and human being, producing the hybrid race, Nephilim.

teronomy 1). These giants were the cause of fear to rise in many within the nation of Israel.

God had always planned to use His nation of Israel as both a light to the world, and an arm of judgment against nations in rebellion against Him, through idolatry, or some other evil. This was the case as Israel prepared to enter Canaan. They were supposed to completely *wipe out* and destroy all people because the Nephilim line had obviously made a comeback since the days of Noah. Given that this was the case, there was a very distinct danger that it had infected everything in Canaan. Nothing was to remain alive.

When the Nephilim perished in the global flood, their bodies died, but *not* their spirits. Their spirits roamed around trying to find other physical bodies to live in and this could well extend to the animal kingdom. We have an excellent example of this in Christ's day. When He cast out the demoniac at Gadarenes, He allowed the demons – named *Legion* – to inhabit the herd of swine nearby. Apparently, these spirits hate not having a body in which to dwell, (cf. Matt 8; Mark 5; Luke 8). Because of their ability to possess and infect with evil, God had every reason and right to use Israel as His physical arm of judgment against these nations as they entered His land.

However, even when the children of Israel *did* enter the Land after wandering for forty years, they still did not do what God wanted as they moved into Canaan. Because of that, the Philistines, as one example, continued to live in the land. It was not until a number of generations later that David went against Goliath, who was said to be roughly nine feet, six inches tall, and he was considered the smaller of his brothers!

Armchair Quarterbacking is Easy
We can play armchair quarterback, and believe that Israel's aggression was reprehensible, but the truth of the matter is that they were under direct orders from God, for God's sovereign purposes. Moses

makes this abundantly clear toward the end of the book of Numbers. To *reprimand* Israel for their actions is to reprimand *God*.

At least part of the reason for God's direction to destroy these people had to do with the corruption of the human race through the introduction of this hybrid species (angel and human), both *before* and *after* the global flood. Even though God dealt with this first occurrence through the event of the global flood, it appears that they began to rise up again and were already *waiting* for Israel by the time they reached Canaan. It is clear that Satan had been busy for centuries attempting to thwart God's plans once again where Israel is concerned.

In light of today's teachings espoused by Replacement Theology and Preterism, it is becoming increasingly clear that the position of Anti-Zionism seems to have its origin in the same source as the one who has attempted to destroy God's plans from the beginning; Satan himself. However, Satan's modus operandi is to use these individuals to viciously attack the Christian Zionist for advocating support for God's special people and Israel's future.

Of course, Anti-Zionists bristle at the suggestion that the view they hold may, in fact, be Anti-Semitic. The possibility *must* be considered and investigated.

Chapter 5
Replacing the Truth?

Replacement Theology (as well as Covenant Theology and Preterism), postulates that Israel has been *replaced* by the Church. Therefore, Israel exists no more, they say. She is gone, done, kaput. Because Israel rejected her Messiah, ultimately crucifying Him, God's patience had run out (their view), and due to this, He utterly abandoned Israel, permanently casting them aside. In this author's opinion, the eyes of the individuals who believe this remain closed to the truth.

This is an unfortunate position to accept as true, because as mentioned, it appears to be completely *unbiblical.* There is really nothing in Scripture (if Scripture is allowed to speak for itself), that lends support to this current and errant view of God's dealings with either the Church or Israel. Quite the opposite is the truth, in fact.

If we consider all the times that Israel wholly failed God by refusing to believe Him, which led to rebellion and disobedience, we *never* see a time when God cast Israel away from Himself *permanently*. God always emphasized His faithfulness in spite of Israel's disobedience. Yet, we are to now believe that God finally came to a point of realizing that continuing with Israel was hopeless, so He abandoned them, creating a new entity instead from which there would be no difference between the Jew or Gentile, man or woman, free or slave.

God, the Breaker of Promises
Unfortunately, it appears that this view tends to make Jehovah the God who reneges on His promises. In this case, the promises were stated to Abraham not once, but on at least three separate occasions, and then to others who came after Abraham as well.

Theologians who believe that God tossed Israel aside do so based on Israel's rejection of Jesus as Messiah. However, it is clear from the Old Testament alone, that the Messiah was to be rejected and would die as a direct result of that rejection (cf. Isaiah 53). Since God saw, knew, and even designed this to occur, it is impossible to believe that this rejection of Christ was God's "final straw." This is especially difficult to grasp considering the fact that God made the specific promises to Abraham that were unconditional (though the Covenant Theologian views these as *conditional* promises), and He saw everything before anything came to fruition. Clearly, the Gentiles would benefit (all the families of the earth will be blessed through Abraham; Genesis 12:1-3), and this benefit refers to *salvation*. The other promises made to Abraham were specifically made for the future nation of Israel and cannot, nor should be transferred to the Church.

Isaiah 53, Daniel 9, and numerous other portions of Scripture clearly indicate that the Messiah was to be killed, long before it happened. We also note that every time Israel rejected God in some way, His judgment always came. This was the reason Israel (the southern kingdom), was in captivity in Babylon in the book of Daniel. Israel had rejected God, refusing to comply with His rule over them.

Every time Israel rejects God through some form of rebellion, God sends judgment. This was usually accomplished by God prompting a neighboring empire to sweep in, and destroy much of Israel's population. Any remaining Israelites would be taken alive as slaves. This happened time and time again. Israel was normally tossed, chased, or carried out of their own land. Israelites were then dispersed into the world among their captives and foreign nations.

Eventually though, God always brought them back to their own Land, and to the city of Jerusalem, God's center of the world. There is no reason to believe that God always intended at one point, to drop Israel forever. Scripture unmistakably indicates otherwise.

One Rejection After Another
Israel's path has always been a cycle of obedience to God, then rejection of Him. From there, Israel would be overcome by a foreign entity, taken captive, and led out of the Land. After a time, they cried out to God (usually a new generation of Jews), and God would 'open His ears.' He then rescued Israel from her captives, bringing her back to her homeland. That is the cycle and in essence, they are in a "dispersion" part of that cycle now, though we can see throughout the world, since 1948, that Jewish people have begun making their way back to Israel. However, in this current case, it is noteworthy to understand that though this author believes God is responsible for bringing them back to the land, the Israelites themselves are unaware of it. They have not called out to Him. They are merely being brought back to the Land (cf. Ezekiel 20), for God's purposes.

It is important to note, that every time Israel was judged by God, it was done because of their *rejection of* Him as King over Israel. This was first done by demanding to have a human king over them, and resulted in the ordination of Saul to that office, the first of many kings (cf. 1 Samuel). God knew they were rejecting Him and His rule.

Every time judgment occurred with Israel, it occurred because of their rejection of God. That rejection was normally seen in the form of idolatry, or by disobedience to other laws that God had given to the nation. All of it resulted from Israel's rejection of God.

The same is true during Jesus' time. He appeared on this planet in the form of a baby, grew up among His own Jewish people, ministered to them for roughly three years in a public ministry, and was then executed, by crucifixion. Israel's rejection of God had occurred again when Israel's leaders *rejected* Jesus. There is nothing new here at all. It was always the same rejection of God, this time, culminating in the rejection of the Messiah, God in the flesh.

In spite of this, many would have us believe that this rejection of Jesus was something different, which caused the nation of Israel to go beyond God's ability to forgive. This left God with no choice but to permanently cast Israel off as His favored nation.

This is absolute nonsense, as Israel *always* rejected God in one form or another when it came to that part of the cycle. We are to believe that this particular act of rejecting God in Jesus somehow pushed God over the edge? We are to believe that God looked at Israel and said; *"All those times in the past, when rejecting my commands, and my love, they were rejecting Me as Ruler over them. This final time, they have rejected my commands, my love, and Me as Ruler (through my Son). That's it! I've had it with Israel! I will forget them forever!"* What happened to His mercies endure forever (cf. Psalm 136)?

The Anti-Zionist wants us to believe that this rejection of Jesus Christ was so dire that it trumped any prior rejection of God. However, the truth of the matter is that *all* rejections of God by Israel were in the same category; *rejection of God.* There is *no* difference. Rejecting God is rejecting *God.* There are not *degrees* to rejecting God. A person does not reject God just a little, or quite a lot. Rejecting God is rejecting God.

The Birth of Replacement Theology
At this point, let us review a few more comments from the Christian Action for Israel. *"One of the factors that led to the birth of Replacement Theology was an historic one. This teaching was birthed at a time when Israel as a nation was in dispersion. The Land of Canaan was barren, infertile and her cities, especially Jerusalem, were mere desert outposts. The devastation was complete and it seemed beyond belief that the Land could ever again be restored to its former glory.*

The impossibility of the situation led to a false re-interpretation of God's Word. Christendom has since paid the price. For God confounded her unbelief in 1948 with the restoration of the State of Israel and exposed the tragic and wicked fruits of Replacement Theology. Christian Zionists are determined to proclaim the truth of the New Testament, namely that God is not finished with Israel and that, in fact, she will yet become a "cornerstone" of His plan for the world.

Thirdly, Christian Zionists recognise with sorrow and repentance the role that many Christians have played in the persecution of the Jewish People. This is even more disturbing since all we love and enjoy as Christians came from them (Romans 9:1-5). In the light of this awful reality they seek to be a blessing and source of comfort to Zion (Isaiah 40:1-2).[25]

---

[25] http://christianactionforisrael.org/4thcongress2.html

A Bit of History

History has shown that many within Christendom viewed the 1948 event of Israel's statehood, with shock and incredulity. It nowhere fits *their* understanding of God's dealings with Israel. Because they firmly believed then (and now), that Israel was entirely and permanently rejected *by* God, the fact that she is now a state can be nothing more than an accident of nature.

If not for the United Nations (we are told by Anti-Zionists), Israel would not have had a chance to gain her current statehood. In so doing, the United Nations is guilty of forcing untold thousands of Arabs to deal with "their" land being given away with a "take it or leave it" ultimatum.

Anti-Zionists are convinced that the continued unrest in the Middle East today is due *solely* to Israel's presence and aggression. The Jewish people have *no* business being there as a state again. (In fact, I personally know Jewish believers who hold this tragic view.) If they just went there to live, that would be one thing, but they went there to live *and* to become a sovereign state. This was the catalyst that created unrest and untold difficulties for Arabs because of Israel's provocation.

It is absolutely true that the Land of Canaan in 1948 was in large measure, completely desolate. Nothing was growing, and dirt and dust went on for miles and miles. Any Arabs who *did* live there, existed as Bedouins, with their families and herds moving from place to place as the weather and seasons dictated, in order to survive.

Once Jewish people began relocating back to Israel however, things began to change. The once barren and desolate fields and valleys were transformed into gardens of oases everywhere. Kibbutzim sprang up here and there with no walls to protect these new communities. When they took up residence, the Jewish people *changed* the land as if God's blessing was once again upon them.

This needs to be understood. Israel as a land, was essentially lying vacant, and it was not until the people of Israel began to relocate back to it, and renovate many areas within Israel, that it suddenly became something that Arabs wanted for themselves.

Yassar Arafat also took advantage of the situation by artificially *creating* a culture of Arab people he called *Palestinians*. Prior to this PR campaign of Arafat's, *anyone* and *everyone* who lived in that area was referred to as Palestinian. This applied to Jews as well as Arabs and other Gentiles.

Yessir Yassar

Yassar Arafat was successful in singling out Arabs, as if *they* were the only ones to rightly to be called Palestinian. This gave them a decided advantage because it began to appear to the world that these Arabs – now Palestinians – were already well ensconced in that geographical area. It began to appear as though the Jews, who were now coming back to Canaan in large numbers, were in fact, *displacing* people who actually *belonged* there. This was *not* true.

In an article by Karen Russo, quoting Prime Minister Golda Meier, she writes, *"There was no such thing as Palestinians. They never existed… It wasn't as though there was a Palestinian people in Palestine, then [Jewish settlers] came, threw them out and took their country away from them. They didn't exist."*[26]

Russo continues with, *"Palestine was Yassar Arafat's brainchild. Born in Egypt, Arafat believes his talents were wasted as a civil engineer in Kuwait. Having helped form the Fatah party in 1957, Arafat decided they could be the basis of a new nation, one he would control. A nation called 'Palestine.' Under his nom de guerre, Abu Ammar, Arafat led dozens of raids against the Israelis, eventually turning his rag-tag group of Fatah terrorists into the very first 'Palestinians.' Ethnically*

---

[26] Karen Russo, *The Greatest PR Scam in History* (Sacramento Union, February 15, 2008)

and culturally, they were Syrians, Iraqis, Lebanese and Saudis – 'Jordanians' if you wish, but Jordan didn't exist as a geographical unit 1949. Today, 'Palestinians' are indistinguishable from any other Arabs. They have no distinct language, religion, history, or tradition. Before Arafat, there had never been a 'Palestinian' leader. There's never been a country called 'Palestine'."[27]

It would be helpful at this juncture to discover what the apostle Paul teaches about Israel and whether or not there is any possibility of a future for them as a nation. As we have discussed, it is known from the book of Acts that Paul (Saul prior to his salvation), met Christ on the road to Damascus (cf. Acts 9). He was on a mission sanctioned by the religious leaders of Israel to chase down and bring back (or have executed) any Jews, who had become followers of "The Way" (a derogatory term for Christianity at that time in history). This is what Paul was in the process of accomplishing as he headed toward Damascus.

When Paul's life was transformed by Jesus on that road, he not only became a follower of Him, but completely dedicated his life from that moment on, to evangelizing the lost, starting with Jewish people. The lost, as far as Paul was concerned, were found in the Jews of Israel. He also realized that the gospel was to go out to the Gentiles as well, and it was in this order that he presented the gospel; to the Jew first and also to the Gentile. Though some try to argue otherwise, Paul never varied his methods.

It is clear from a number of statements Paul makes, that his knowledge of Jesus Christ came directly from Jesus Himself. This form of revelation was special to Paul, as it should be. He claimed he built on no one else's ministry and even what he was taught came directly from Jesus, not from any of the other apostles (Galatians

---

[27] Karen Russo, *The Greatest PR Scam in History* (Sacramento Union, February 15, 2008)

1:12; 2:2). It was because of his tremendous understanding of Scripture (the Old Testament, or T'nach), that Jesus taught and revealed to Paul the truths *behind* the text, of which many ultimately referred to Him as Messiah.

These divine revelations were the foundational basis for Paul's ministry. With respect to God's revelations to Paul, it was Paul, who first spoke of the Church as being a mystery (cf. Romans 16:25; Galatians 3:23; Ephesians 3:3, 5). It is clear from Paul's teaching that nothing like the Church was known prior to Christ.

Replacement Theology in the Batter's Box
Replacement Theology has an interesting (albeit wrong), way of getting around this. They say that God had *always* meant for the gospel to be extended to the Gentiles. Therefore, it was not a true mystery, since it was known from the Old Testament that the gospel would always go out to the Gentiles. However, the mystery that Paul spoke of was in making the "two men one" which is what occurs during the regeneration process alike for Jews and Gentiles. The Church is nowhere to be found in the Old Testament, or prior to Paul revealing that mystery, for that matter.

I know of no one who denies that the Old Testament teaches that the gospel was to be extended to the Gentiles. Unfortunately, Anti-Zionists are confusing the fact of the gospel being extended to the Gentiles, and the creation of the Church. Paul is speaking specifically of the Church, which would include people of all cultures and nations and was completely separate from the nation of Israel. The Church was *nowhere* indicated in the Old Testament.

The fact that we see from the Old Testament (Genesis 12:1-3), that the gospel *would* be extended to the Gentiles, does *not* mean that the Old Testament prophets knew of the *eventual* establishment of the Church. They most likely understood that the gospel would be extended to the Gentiles *through* the nation of Israel.

There was actually no reason for God to reveal this aspect of His plan to the prophets of the OT, and for one extremely good reason: Had God revealed any aspect of the Church, or even *hinted* at it in the Old Testament, that knowledge would have *also been* revealed to *Satan*. Had Satan known about the Church, it is extremely likely that he would have done things markedly different before and during the lifetime of Christ on earth.

Satan was obviously aware of Jesus' birth from the Old Testament Scriptures, and he also knew where that birth would take place. He attempted to work through Herod to destroy Christ before He could grow up and go to the cross. Instead, an untold number of innocent babies were brutally murdered by Roman soldiers. Numerous times throughout Christ's earthly life, Satan attempted to incite the religious leaders of Israel to kill Jesus, which would have been before His appointed time.

Had Satan known about the church, he most assuredly would have done all he could to have stopped Christ from being crucified. Knowledge of the Church would have given him knowledge of many other things. Putting two and two together, Satan could have mounted a major campaign against the Church, prior to its inception. Certainly, he would have tried to stop its birth. As it was (and is), he had to make do with his constant attempts of introducing error into the Church.

God kept the mystery of the Church all to Himself. This group of believers taken from all nations and cultures, makes up one Body, and one Bride, for Jesus Christ.

So while the Anti-Zionist believes, and diligently argues, that the Church was known in the Old Testament, Scripture proves otherwise. Had it not been a real *mystery*, Paul would never have referred to it as such. While we know (from the OT), that the gospel was to go out to the Gentiles, there is nothing there, which teaches, or explains the *essence* of the Church; the idea of all being made complete in Christ with no differentiation between gender or ethnicity *is* the Church.

However, what else does the Anti-Zionist believe that conflicts with biblical authority? Just as importantly, where did these particular views and teachings start?

Origen

For most students of church history, just mentioning the name *Origen* is enough to provide the answer. Most know of his proclivity to allegorize, though he was possibly one of the most educated men of the early Church fathers.

History tells us that he was born in Alexandria around A.D. 186 and died in A.D. 254. Most of the documents he composed were written between the years A.D. 204 to 232.

Because of Alexander the Great, the city of Alexandria had become the main seat of Greek learning due to its literature. The Greek influence had spread over the known world. *"It was also the chief seat of Christian theology until it was taken over by Arabs in 641 A.D."*[28]

Origen was a tremendous scholar and writer. The main problem though was his method of interpretation (if it can be called that). He believed that *"scripture admits of a three-fold interpretation corresponding to the tripartite nature of man: the 'bodily' (the literal or historical); the 'psychical' (the ethical); and the 'pneumatic' (the allegorical or mystical)."*[29] Here we have a deeply committed man of faith who had apparently worked out a system of theology that was so convoluted, even he became confused at times!

---

[28] Derek White, *Replacement Theology: Its Origin, History and Theology* (East Sussex: CFI Communications 1997), 5
[29] Ibid, 6

Many scholars and commentators who came well after Origen did not speak highly of him. In one particular writing related to Israel, Origen states without equivocation *"We may thus assert in utter confidence that the Jews will not return to their earlier situation, for they have committed the most abominable of crimes in forming this conspiracy against the Savior of the human race..."*[30]

Unfortunately, for Origen, and those who believe as he did, it is no secret that the A.D. 70 destruction of Jerusalem was the direct result of Israel's rejection of Christ. However, *that* was the judgment, along with being once again dispersed. There is nothing in the Olivet Discourse indicating that the Jews would never return to the Land to repossess it. The only way this can be understood from Scripture is by allegorizing various biblical texts. More often than not, Scripture is allegorized by the *interpreter's* choice, not because the text actually insists upon it.

In the case of Origen, we have an individual who was very close to the first century churches, yet came up with a system of interpretation that is plainly absurd. The system he developed must be avoided if for no other reason than the fact that interpreter becomes the subjective source of truth revealed in Scripture.

Development of Replacement Theology
It is very easy to see how this Replacement Theology came into development. By the second century, the Church was left trying to determine its identity, since it was made up of both Jews and Gentiles by this point. In some areas, it created a major identity crisis, and the answer was determined to be in what Origen had stated, which became known as Replacement Theology.

Augustine carried the idea forward, and it became an integral part of Roman Catholic doctrine. This theology prompted an attitude of

---
[30] Ibid, 6-7

blame toward the Jews, as individuals and as a people group. From this point on, the covenant in Jeremiah 31 was seen to *exclude* Jews. Upon searching the writings of the Church fathers from this era of time, it is exceedingly rare to find even reference to Paul's teaching on the ultimate redemption of Israel. Just because this belief of the early Church fathers was so prevalent, it does not make it a *correct* belief.

The Church had become the new Israel. All the blessings that were previously given *to* Israel, were now applied to, and appropriated by, the Church. It was not long before the total culture of Judaism was literally wiped entirely away from the Bible, and from the Church itself.

In the end then, two major concepts encapsulated Replacement Theology:

1. *"All the premises and encouragements provided in the Old Testament are exclusively the property of the Church, which is now the true 'Israel."*
2. *Israel has been completely disinherited and excluded. Furthermore, the formerly 'good' elements of Judaism have become 'evil' since Christ's coming."*[31]

From that point onward, it became very easy to not only treat the Jewish people as if they were disinherited by God, but to actually *negate* them, as if they had never even been God's chosen people at all!

Many early Church fathers displayed a clear disregard for the Jews, including Jerome, Ambrose, Augustine, and Chrysostom. The latter typified the hatred that had developed by that time with the

---

[31] Derek White, *Replacement Theology: Its Origin, History and Theology* (East Sussex: CFI Communications 1997), 8

statement *"When it is clear that God hates (the Jew), it is the duty of Christians to hate them too."*

In essence, this Replacement Theology is founded upon two things; 1) terrible hermeneutics, leading to a wrong interpretation of Scripture, and 2) hatred for the Jew. Is it any wonder that this led to the sizeable amount of anti-Semitism that has occurred throughout the past? The historical landscape is filled with events, incidents and even a way of life in which the Jewish person has been vilified, made null and void, and even cursed!

All of this was deliberately perpetrated by the Roman Catholic Church, which officially came into existence toward the end of the third century. Their anti-Semitism was and remains obvious, with their inquisitions, crusades, pogroms and other persecutions. Is it any wonder Jewish individuals like Rashi, having grown up in that environment, became an ardent defender of Judaism and the Jew, denouncing the atrocities committed against his people by those who called themselves Christian? Christians of all denominations should be ashamed, as there is no excuse for what has taken place in God's Name against Jewish people. Replacement Theology and Preterism simply provide a vehicle which continues the anti-Semitic rhetoric.

Even during and after the Reformation, people like Luther (though successfully distancing himself from the error of salvation by faith plus works), was unable to extricate himself from the anti-Semitic rancor he held for the Jew. This same anti-Semitism has been pointed out by many since then, to no real avail.

Without this history of anti-Semitic vehemence, it is doubtful that Hitler would have been able to do what he did. Too many Christians stood by either watching, or ignoring the atrocities altogether. They literally buried their heads in the sand as millions of Jewish people were illegally incarcerated, then either gassed, or burned to death! How is *any* of that Christian?!

We could spend more time explaining how the Christian Church divorced herself completely from her Jewish roots, but it is likely that the picture has been made clear. Anti-Semitism is an extremely ugly part of the Church's history. It stands there until the end of time as an example of the type of brutality that can be perpetrated on innocent people. The Church should be ashamed, and those who are not, while referring to themselves as Christian are as guilty as those who did the deeds. The saddest part of all this is that anti-Semitism continues to exist through people like the Anti-Zionist, who sees no need for Jews or Israel. Because of that terrible deed of rejecting Christ, to His crucifixion, there is absolutely no forgiveness for the Jew, or Israel, we are told by the Anti-Zionist.

Unfortunately, at the same time the Anti-Zionist is telling us that the Jew is "past tense," as is Israel, they are busy accusing the Christian Zionist of *excusing* the Jew for crucifying Christ. In essence, the Christian Zionist is made to appear as though he is aiding and abetting the Jew in this crime of murdering Jesus.

Both Jews AND Gentiles Are Guilty!
Here is the actual reality that the Replacement Theologian, Covenant Theologian, and Anti-Zionist have completely missed. No *one* group is guilty of perpetrating the crime of murder against Jesus Christ. *Both* Jew *and* Gentile played a role in Christ's death. The fault does not lie exclusively with the Jew as the Anti-Zionist would have us believe. While all people share the guilt and culpability of putting Christ to death, God's sovereignty completely oversaw the situation, allowing Christ to be put to death. This was done in order that salvation would become available. It must be stressed though, that just as Judas played a part in putting Christ on the cross, according to God's specific plans, he is still fully culpable for his actions.

Yes, it was the group of religious leaders of Jesus' day, called the Sanhedrin, who brought charges against Jesus. He of course was completely innocent of those charges, but no one (Jew or Gentile), rose to His defense. Since these religious leaders could not put Him to death themselves, they needed the government of Rome to do it, so it was they turned to Pontus Pilate.

Rome, through Pilate, originally wanted nothing to do with Jesus. Pilate knew that Jesus was not a threat to Roman rule. He found nothing evil in Him and relayed his findings to the religious leaders of Israel. Not satisfied with Pilate, they demanded that Jesus be crucified.

Even Pilate's wife warned him that he should have nothing to do with Christ's trial at all. He should have listened to her. Pilate – a Gentile – was the one who pronounced sentence and to make matters worse, he had Christ scourged prior to the execution. While this was the custom, since Pilate knew that Christ was innocent of the charges, one has to wonder why he felt he needed to include scourging in the process. Yes, it was prophesied that Christ would suffer the pain and humiliation of scourging (cf. Isaiah 53). However, Pilate suffers the condemnation for going ahead with that decision.

The Roman soldiers (also Gentile), brutally scourged Christ after they tied him to the wooden post, completely stripping Him of His clothing. In all likelihood, there was one Roman soldier on each side of Christ, taking turns raining down the brutal beating, one after the other. How many lashes Christ received is not clear, as much of it was left up to the sadism of the individual soldiers. When they grew tired, or bored, they would stop.

Once Christ had been thoroughly flogged, He was then roughly forced onto his back, on the ground, with the crossbeam under His head. His hands would have been tied to the crossbeam. The upright stipe was already in the ground on Calvary's hill, silently and resolutely waiting for its next victim.

Once this was accomplished, Christ would be forced to walk nearly one full mile from Jerusalem to Calvary, just outside the city walls. We know from the gospels that He fell enough times during this trek, to warrant someone else to carry His crossbeam.

Arriving at Calvary, He would again be pushed backwards onto the ground. His arms would be spread into a 65 degree angle away from His body and His hands would be nailed to the crossbeam. This nailing was not done to ensure the body would remain on the cross, so much as it was done as an extra measure of sadism. The victim would often also have ropes tied around His arms to the crossbeam. This is what actually kept the victim's wrists from falling off the cross.

Christ's feet were then nailed to the lower portion of the stipe; one foot over the other, so that only one nail was required. Of course, the victim was stripped completely of his clothes; another form of Roman indignity that the soldiers foisted upon their victims.

Once Christ's hands had been fully secured to the crossbeam, He would have then been hoisted up – one Roman soldier on each side – and because of the square hole in the center of the crossbeam, it would simply be placed over the upright stipe, sliding down until the thickness of the wood of the stipe kept it from sliding down further.

It was here, on the cross, that each victim would die. Pictures often depict Christ as being ten or more feet above the crowd. This was not the case. The Romans wanted things done quickly and efficiently. Getting Christ up to that height would have required ladders and a pulley system. Keeping the stipe's height so that it was essentially a little taller than an average man allowed the process to go very quickly. It also put the victim just above the eye level with other individuals who would walk by. Because of this proximity, they could nearly look at the victim directly in his eyes, in person, and taunt him, spit on him, or slap him if they so desired. Crucifixion was an extremely brutal, humiliating way to be executed, and it was one of Rome's favorite techniques.

Let us not forget that, while the Jew brought their charges against Jesus to Pilate, it was the Gentile Pilate and the Gentile Roman soldiers who physically carried out the murder. If we want to consider people by ethnicity, then both Jews and Gentiles are guilty of murdering Jesus Christ. Fortunately for us, it was His death, the shedding of His blood and His resurrection that purchased salvation for us. Without His death, there would be no options. We would all ultimately face the second death in the Lake of Fire.

Ultimately, all those personally involved in that crucifixion process where Jesus is concerned, bear the guilt; Jew and Gentile alike. However, it was for this that Christ came. His death was the price that needed to be paid, in order that we might become free of sin's punishment.

The Jews alone do not bear the guilt. It is spread equally among Jews and Gentiles, across the board. Those who firmly believe that the Jews alone are responsible for killing Christ do not know their Bible at all. However, it certainly appears as though they are all too familiar with racism, in the form of Anti-Semitism, the result of which leads to Anti-Zionism every time.

Kingdom Now or Dominion Theology
"Perhaps the most extreme version of Replacement Theology is known as 'Kingdom Now' or 'Dominion Theology. This teaches that the Church will govern the world and all its systems for Jesus. The Church will thus prepare the world for Him to step down from heaven and receive the reins of government from her."[32]

---

[32] Derek White, *Replacement Theology: Its Origin, History and Theology* (East Sussex: CFI Communications 1997), 18

We see this theology unequivocally embraced by many today. Christians are taught to believe they must be involved in social action issues. The more we can accomplish to reverse all wrongs in society, the sooner Jesus will be able to return to this planet to reign. The emphasis here is on what *humanity* can accomplish. In other words, God's hands are tied, because He is in the position of having to wait while the Church on earth brings the entire earth, with the entire population, under the control, or authority of the Church. Once this has been accomplished, then Jesus will be *able* to return to this world. This is exactly what Roman Catholicism attempted to do, and has, to date, failed to accomplish.

Today's Replacement Theology

Replacement Theology is very similar to its predecessor, in the belief that all promises given to Israel are now to be appropriated by the Church. The chief means of seeing this, is through the process of allegorizing Scripture, thereby removing the literal aspect from it.

To the Replacement Theologian then, this means that the Land of Israel (that God promised to be a possession to Israel *for all time*), is now meant to be the entire earth, in which the Church obeys the Great Commission. It is taught that as more and more people come to a saving knowledge of Jesus Christ, more and more of the earth geographically comes under God's power and authority.

Isaiah 43:5-7, though referring to the regathering of Jews from all parts of the world, is now taken to mean the gathering of all *believers* in Christ from all parts of the world.

Hosea 6:1-2 discusses the future resurrection of Israel, yet for the Replacement Theologian it now refers to Jesus (the *representative* of Israel) having been raised from the dead. So instead of a physical resurrection of the Land of Israel with the Jews possessing it, it now refers to Jesus' resurrection and the future resurrection of those who believe in Him.

Beyond all of this, God specifically promised to David that someone from his house would sit on his throne and his throne would last forever (2 Samuel 7:13; 1 Chronicles 17:1-14). It is now taken to mean that the Church – now spiritual "Israel" – is ruled over by Jesus, the representative from Israel. He now sits on His Father's throne in heaven, and now rules over His people.

Nevertheless, there are some interesting thoughts hidden away from the Replacement Theologian's eyes in the Old Testament. When God made His pronouncement that someone from David's lineage would always sit on his throne, He followed through by providing a ruler from Solomon's branch of David's family for the next four hundred years. In Luke 1:32, in reference to Christ, it says that *"He will be great and will be called the Son of the Most High. And the Lord God will give to him the throne of his father David."*

There is a bit of a parenthesis though, after the four hundred years, and prior to Christ's reign from his father David's throne. Anyone who knows the actual history of Israel as reported in God's Word alone, knows that as time went on, the various kings over Israel had become so evil and corrupt that God had no choice but to remove them. Jeremiah 22:28-30 shows the extent of God's anger toward that line of kings. He decides that there will be no more kings from that line. The last king to reign over Israel was Jehoiachin, also called Jeconiah, and he only reigned for three months!

At first glance, it would *appear* as though God broke His promise to David. Yet, this cannot be the case, since God cannot lie. So what happened? The Replacement Theologian says that the promise was *conditional* and since Israel blew it, God was free to do as He pleased, no longer bound by the terms of the conditional covenant.

However, it seems clear enough that the promise made to David was actually *unconditional* in nature. This is plain enough from the same book of Jeremiah in which God cuts off the royal line to David's throne. Ten chapters *after* chapter twenty-two of Jeremiah, God says this to Jeremiah; *"For thus says the LORD: David shall never lack a man to sit on the throne of the house of Israel,"* (Jeremiah 33:17). He says this *after* He states that there will be no more kings from the royal line in Jeremiah 22. If Scripture is allowed to interpret itself, there is only one feasible way to understand this; that God will continue with a king on David's physical throne. But how?

The evidence of Scripture supports the idea that God's promise to David was completely unconditional. The only "conditional" aspect of it, might be seen in terms of each individual who sat on David's throne. Each could be removed as God saw fit, based on their loyalty to God. This, however, would in no way affect the unconditional promise that God had originally made to David.

Numbers 27:8 indicates how God worked after He chose to cut off the royal line from reigning. *"And you shall speak to the people of Israel, saying, 'If a man dies and has no son, then you shall transfer his inheritance to his daughter'."* Apparently, God chose to continue the royal line through daughters. Jack Kelly, of Grace Thru Faith, comments on this, stating *"At the end of the Book of Numbers an interesting loophole emerged. A man died without a son, leaving [four] daughters. They came to Moses complaining that they would lose the family land since there was no son to inherit it. Moses sought the Lord Who decreed that if there was no son in a family daughters could inherit family land providing they married within their own tribal clan. In effect they had to marry a cousin to keep the land in the 'family.' This made sense since land was allotted first by tribe then by clan then by family. Marrying within the clan kept the families in close proximity and preserved the tribal allotment. (Num. 36 1:13)"*[33]

What is extremely interesting about this is how the Lord worked out this scenario so that Jesus would be born of David's line, yet the

---

[33] http://gracethrufaith.com/childrens-stories-for-adults/the-virgin-mary-had-a-baby-boy/

"curse" God had placed on the royal line in Jeremiah 22, would not affect Christ because of the marriage of Joseph and Mary. Kelly explains, *"When Mary accepted Joseph's offer of marriage she preserved her family's land and also made good her son's claim to the throne of Israel. Jesus was in the royal succession through Joseph but escaped the curse since he wasn't Joseph's biological son. But He was a biological descendant of David's through his mother and therefore of the 'house and lineage of David'."*[34]

Replacement Theology takes Old Testament passages that specifically reference Israel and the promises God made *to* them, and repositions those passages so that they now point *to*, and find *fulfillment* in the Church.

However, a close look at the text of Scripture and especially those repeated by Jesus during His earthly ministry, clearly indicates that to Jesus, these were valid, as yet unfulfilled promises that had been made to Israel. These *would* find their literal fulfillment at some point in future time through Christ physically. Jesus made no attempt to spiritualize or allegorize any of these passages of Scripture. He took them at face value, understanding them with a literal meaning.

A Multitude of Errors Within Replacement Theology
There are a number of glaring errors found within the system of Replacement Theology that need to be understood. These errors show that the Replacement Theologian, far from finding God's will and purposes in their method of interpretation, actually *changes* what God has clearly stated, making His Word mean something else entirely. If this is the case, then the Replacement Theologian comes under judgment for sacrificing the actual meaning of God, for the artificial meaning of man.

---

[34] Ibid

- **Law & Prophets Fulfilled By Jesus** – if, in fact, the Church is now the new Israel, then God has absolutely rejected Israel. This makes no sense in light of Christ's statement that He did not come to destroy the Law and Prophets, but to fulfill them (Matthew 5). He literally promises in Matthew 5 that nothing would pass away until *everything* (even the 'jot' and 'tittle' of Hebrew characters), came to pass.

- **"God has not rejected His people"** – Paul makes this abundantly clear in Romans 11. If God has, in fact, turned away permanently from Israel, why would Paul state that God has not done so? If the context means anything, Paul was undeniably referring to Israel here, not merely individual Jews. It seems obvious that Paul meant what he said, that God has not turned His back on His people.

- **Vindication** – one of the things Replacement Theologians seem to forget is that the major reason God will follow through on His promises is for the sake of His Name (Ezekiel 36, as one example). Because the honor of His Name is so important to Him (and should be to us as well), He *will* defend that Name by regathering Israel. There are many passages in Scripture, which indicate God's displeasure with the way His Name has been dragged through the mud. It was the nation of Israel (the *unbelieving* Jews here), which created this intolerable situation, which required God to send judgment time and time again. Because other nations overcame them, they *assumed* Israel's God had become powerless.

- **No Form or Method** – when looking at the Bible from the viewpoint of Replacement Theology, it quickly becomes apparent that the views understood from Scripture are *read into* the text. On the other hand, the careful interpreter of God's Word approaches the Bible with the question, "What does the Bible *say*?" instead of "What does it mean to *me*?" This is an important difference. The Bible should never be read *into* for meaning, but meaning should always be gained *from* it. Because of this errant approach of tending to read meaning into Scripture, anything that even remotely applies to Israel from the Old Testament is often applied to the Church instead. Well known verses spoken to Israel in the form of promises now become the Church's. This is due only because the Replacement Theologian reads into Scripture, by allegorizing, which is nothing more than Eisegesis.

• **Difference Between the Testaments** – by allegorizing Old Testament texts, which refer to Israel, and applying them to the Church in the New Testament, the separation of these two writings is completely eradicated. In essence, Replacement Theology denies the truth of Scripture, found in its literal meaning, preferring instead an artificial truth that they impose on it. An artificial, or man-made truth is no truth at all.

• **The New Testament** – if we were to substitute the word "Church" with every instance the writers used the word "Israel," it would not make sense. This can only be done when the interpreter allegorizes Scripture.

• **Israel Separate from the Church** – the New Testament makes it abundantly clear that the Church is continually separate from Israel. As Arnold Fruchtenbaum states, the Church has become *partakers* with Israel, not *over* takers (cf. Footsteps of the Messiah). This is a truth that few give heed to anymore. Too many within the Church believe that the Church has completely pushed Israel out of the picture entirely, with the Church having superseded and even become superior to Israel.

• **He Must Be a Liar** – because Replacement Theology *changes* what God has said, it is, in fact, guilty of making a liar out of God. When God promised that Israel would have the land forever, Replacement Theology states that the covenant to Abraham was *conditional.* Since Israel broke that covenant, then God is free from the obligation of fulfilling it. This of course would be true *if* and *only if* it can be proven that the covenant God made with Abraham was actually a conditional covenant. Numerous biblical scholars have easily shown that the covenant was and remains *unconditional* in nature. If it was unconditional in nature, we have no other choice but to say that God broke His promises (if we are to believe that the Church is now Israel). If He could break His promises to Israel, what is to stop Him from breaking promises to the Church, or to individual Christians?

Chapter 6
The Blame Game

It is always remarkable to read a thesis, book or magazine article by those who reek with disdain toward those who deign to support Israel's right to exist as a nation. As mentioned, it is not uncommon to be on the receiving end of all sorts of vicious accusations, because of it. However, it appears that with the growth of Anti-Zionism, the vitriol is coming at a much quicker pace and with more toxicity than before.

C. (Chuck) E. Carlson refers to Christian Zionists as modern day Pharisees. He states, *"The Pharisees of today have moved heaven and earth to discourage thousands of pastors and televangelists from teaching what Jesus said so clearly. The godfather of the Biblical cen-*

sors is the powerfully promoted Scofield study Bible, first printed in England in 1908, but sold in America. Scofield's Study Bible is a traditional, difficult to read, King James version, doctored with hundred of easy to read added notes and inserted descriptive chapter and verse headings. Most of the notes are about the "rapture" the "end times" and the return of the ancient tribe of Israelites to the Holy land. But there are no meaningful notes about Pharisaism.[35]

It All Goes Back to Scofield...Again

It is not at all difficult to determine from where this individual is coming. However, I must admit that I had never heard of Dr. Scofield's study Bible referred to as "the godfather of the Biblical censors." Overall, I find Carlson's comments to be ludicrous.

One of Carlson's comments quoted above turns out to be a complete *fabrication* when he states: "*Most of the notes are about the 'rapture' the 'end times' and the return of the ancient tribe of Israelites to the Holy Land.*" I apologize for my candor, but there is unfortunately no other way to describe it without being thoroughly rude. I have my own copy of the 1909 version of the Scofield Study System Bible (Red Letter Edition). It had already been available to the public for eight years, when published in 1909.

Dr. Scofield's notes effectively begin with his *Introduction* found on page *iii*. In it, he outlines the nature of his notes, (what he refers to as "helps"), what they cover, and the reason for their inclusion. His overall emphasis appears to be on God's sovereignty as seen in part, though not entirely, through God's work of salvation. What is interesting to me is that, by and large, the average Dispensationalist *always* sees God's primary purpose as that of establishing His sovereignty.

---

[35] http://www.whtt.org/articles/020116.htm

On page *v* of his introductory helps, Dr. Scofield includes the article, *A Panoramic View of the Bible.* He speaks of the fact that the Bible is one book, yet is a book of books. He breaks the Bible down into five parts: Preparation (Old Testament), Manifestation (the Gospels), Propagation (the Acts), Explanation (the Epistles), and Consummation (the Apocalypse). When I studied at Philadelphia College of Bible (a college noted for its Dispensational viewpoint), in the mid-1970s, the doctrines found within the entire Bible were taught, not merely the "rapture," or "end times" as C. E. Carlson would have us believe.

Scofield's helps in the Old Testament rarely mention anything about the end times or the rapture and do so *only* when that subject is referenced in the biblical text. Scofield spends the appropriate amount of time discussing the various Dispensations, again though, as they come up in Scripture. This is no different than the Covenant Theologian taking the time to discuss the various Covenants which his system utilizes.

Scofield's helps throughout the Bible are actually fairly sparse, if we compare them to the study notes found in today's Bibles. Many of his notes, far from being captivated with the end times, or the rapture, link many passages of the Old Testament to Christ Himself. He usually does this when encountering Messianic prophecies.

Perusing the Scofield Study System Bible, one finds that it is not uncommon to travel across 20, 50, or even 100 pages before arriving at *one* of Scofield's notes. Scofield also includes an introduction to each of the individual books of the Bible, both Old and New Testaments, as many Bible versions do today. Included in the introduction is normally a brief outline of the entire book.

Certainly, when Isaiah, Daniel, Ezekiel, Joel, Jeremiah, or other books of similar nature are dealt with by Scofield, his notes deal with the Remnant of Israel and various aspects of the end times. This is primarily because Isaiah and Jeremiah both deal with the end times. In other portions of Scripture where he explains the end times theme, it should surprise no one that he does so at the appropriate times; the Olivet Discourse, I and II Thessalonians, a number of passages in books like Romans, Jude, and of course the entire book of Revelation. How can Scofield be faulted for discussing or commenting on subjects which he (and many others), believes the Bible teaches?

The Covenant or Replacement Theologian prefers to believe that the "end times" occurred in A. D. 70 and Christ "returned" spiritually at that time as well. This does not make them correct, and the burden of proof is on them to establish their position beyond doubt from the Bible.

Scofield Drops the Ball on Pharisaism?

Carlson also makes the comment, that *"there are no meaningful notes about Pharisaism."* Apparently though, Carlson missed this note culled directly from Scofield's Study System Bible, *"The Pharisees were strictly a sect. A member was "chaber" (i.e. "knit together," Jud. 20. 11), and took an obligation to remain true to the principals of Pharisaism. They were correct, moral, zealous, and self-denying, but self-righteous (Lk. 18. 9), and destitute of the sense of sin and need (Lk. 7. 39). They were the foremost persecutors of Jesus Christ and the objects of His unsparing denunciation (e.g. Mt. 23. 13-29; Lk. 11. 42, 43)."*[36]

Maybe it is just me, but the above quote seems fairly meaningful in content. What does Carlson expect, that Scofield was supposed to repeat this information, or state something new about the Pharisees every time that sect appeared on the pages of the Bible? Scofield deals with the Pharisees when they *first* appear in the New Testament, in Matthew 5 as noted above. I suppose Scofield could have restated the same information in a different way, thereby emphasiz-

---

[36] C. I. Scofield, *Scofield Study System Bible* (New York Oxford University Press 1909), 996

ing the futility of their thinking and the fact that Christ really, *really, REALLY* denounced them.

The certainty is that Scofield pulled no punches with the Pharisees. He explained who they were, what they did and how their lives were a constant affront to Jesus. Though his explanation of Pharisaism is concise, he did not hold anything back.

What? Nothing About Pharisees?
Carlson continues with *"most Bible commentaries and concordances avoid any serious treatment of how they operate to control civil government, and who their successors are today."*[37] I am not sure how that would be determined. However, there *is* quite a bit of information on the Pharisees available today; at least as much as is *known* about the Pharisees. This particular sect arose during the Intertestamental period (probably during the Maccabbean Revolt, circa 165 B.C.) and died out sometime toward the end of the first century A.D. They were noted for their legalistic view of Scripture. They had so refined it, that they buried the truth. Because of this, they were unable to enter the narrow gate for salvation, and they kept others from doing so as well. Their legalism paraded itself as righteousness, yet their righteousness was far from righteous. They believed that because they were Jews, and because they had the Law of Moses, the Temple and the city of Jerusalem, their salvation was sure.

Apparently, C. E. Carlson made these comments in an article in 2002. I did some searching and came up with over 20 books written about the historical sect of the Pharisees and these were published before 2002. In fact, some date back to 1946.

Carlson concludes his harangue by stating *"Jerry Falwell, Pat Robertson, Jack Van Empe (sic) and dozens more like them have made careers by promoting Israel as a political state and a chosen race. Thousands of*

---

[37] http://www.whtt.org/articles/020116.htm

local church leaders are following this example. Many of these self-professed Christian leaders are the Pharisees of today, achieving fame and influence by pleasing the media secular Zionist media powers."[38] These he refers to as the *"Promoters of Israeli Pharisaism."* The trouble is that Carlson seems to be confused about what constitutes a Pharisee. As we have seen, *legalism* is the main component in the Pharisaical mindset. However, Carlson equates being a Pharisee with "achieving fame and influence by pleasing the media secular Zionist media powers." While the Pharisees of Christ's day were certainly interested in being recognized in the synagogues by the common person, the fact that some of today's Christian leaders are known by the media does not automatically equate them with the legalistic mindset of the Pharisee. In fact, a strong case could be made to show that Carlson himself, is likely more of a Pharisee than those he confuses with being one.

In another part of this resource, the statement is made (as an apologetic of sorts, regarding the beliefs of a person named Sherry) *"While Celebrity leaders usually stop short of stating that salvation itself depends upon the love of Israel, they imply otherwise. The words and actions of men like Falwell, Robertson, Graham and Hagee imply it so strongly; it is no wonder Sherry has come to believe it. And because she believes it so strongly, she says with total confidence* **that love for Israel and the Jews characterizes all true Christians**."[39] (emphasis added)

This accusation apparently means that Christian Zionists believe salvation includes loving the Jews of Israel. If not, then that individual's salvation is in question. If a so-called Christian *hates* or *despises* Jewish people as a group (or even as individuals), then how is it possible that this particular individual can truly be a Christian?

---

[38] http://www.whtt.org/articles/020116.htm
[39] http://www.whtt.org/articles/010411pw.htm

Salvation is from God alone, by faith alone, in Christ alone. *Nothing* is added to salvation. Christ's work on Calvary is the *sole* means by which salvation is available. There is no requirement to love Israel or the Jews in order to *receive* salvation. Loving the brethren is something that occurs *after* and *pursuant to* the salvation that exists *within* the Christian. Love stems from a true conversion to God in Christ. It does not necessarily precede it and the Bible clearly states that Christians should love *all* people, and *especially* those of God's house (Christians). Despite this, it seems apparent, that the Anti-Zionist loves all people *except* Jewish individuals and those Christians, who support Israel.

It is patently clear that the Anti-Zionist has *no* love for Israel, for the Jews, *or* for Christian Zionists. Carlson pointedly remarks that "*Judeo-Christianity. . .is politicized Judaism within the Christian church; it is not Christianity. It is, in fact, anti-Christian--which is why it distorts Christ's words.*"

A quick trip to Carlson's website reveals articles with titles like:

- *Christian Zionists Snap at the Heels of A Man From Galilee*
- *Hamas, The Best Chance for Peace in the Land of the Philistines*
- *Humble and Contrite Thieves: Goldman Sachs wants to pay back 25% and walk away*
- *Israel's Death Culture, a Dragging Anchor*
- *'Christians' Tour Israel: Gaza Extermination Grinds On*
- *Israel's American Apologist for Palestinian Extermination*
- *Evangelical Zionist's Dilemma: Love Your Enemy or Starve Him*
- *ISRAEL: The New American Idol*
- *Christian Zionism Is On The National Council of Churches Radar Screen*
- *The Lie That Justifies Mass Murder: "Hamas Hit Us First"*
- *The Roots of Christian Zionism Part I, The Cause of the Conflict*
- *House Divided: Christian Zionism Agonizes Family Members*

- *Christian Zionist's End Times: Election Reveals Cracks In Logic*
- *Israel knows that peace just doesn't pay*

There are many articles like the ones listed above on Carlson's website. It is obviously a website that Hitler himself would have been proud to have been associated with. The hatred of Jews is palpable in many of these articles, yet they have the temerity to refer to the Christian Zionist as racist.

911 and the FBI

It is not uncommon to come face to face with the general Anti-Zionist belief that 9/11 was not perpetrated by Islam extremists, but by *Jews*! According to these Anti-Zionists, Jews are responsible for taking down the World Trade Center towers, not Islamic terrorists. What *were* we thinking? These same Anti-Zionists refer to the FBI as the chief terrorist organization of the world in an article titled, *"See the handiwork of the world's leading terrorist organization, the FBI"*[40]

It is difficult to understand how labeling the FBI as the world's leading terrorist organization is not somehow, how shall we say, *anti-American*, or in their vernacular, being a traitor to America? They have their view for justifying their position, which in their mind, keeps them from being a traitor to the United States. The truth belies their own deceit, however.

Dispensationalism is the Root of All Evil

While perusing many other sites dedicated to crushing the evil Christian Zionist, it appears to be common place to read these types of sentiments, *"In order to fulfill Biblical prophecy, Dispensationalists have been working hard to ensure that the world's Jews return to Israel and occupy all of Palestine. To facilitate that process, Dispensationalists have been leading groups of pilgrims to Israel since Falwell's first*

---

[40] http://www.public-action.com/911/chrzion.html#EXTINCT

visit in order to win financial and political support for the Jewish settlements in the West Bank and Gaza Strip," or "Christian Zionists Are Premillennialists. Of the many theories about when Christ will return, the most popular is called premillennial dispensationalism."

As we can see, for the Anti-Zionist, it all comes down to a blatant disregard, and abject hatred for Dispensationalism. This is not unusual for church-goers today of the Covenant Theology or Replacement Theology position. Dispensationalism has been inaccurately critiqued and reviewed since the early 1950s when John Gerstner first charged that Dispensationalism teaches two methods of salvation; *grace plus works* in the Old Testament and *grace alone* in the New Testament. Of course, this belief is a complete misunderstanding by opponents of Dispensationalism, but it makes no difference to those who oppose Dispensationalism. They prefer to believe the misrepresentation that Gerstner voiced. Irrespective of how often attempts are made to correct the wrong beliefs of others concerning Dispensationalism, nothing changes. It is almost as if the Anti-Zionists do not want it to change. If they did, who would they complain about?

Racism in Dispensationalism?
In another article written against Dispensationalism by Thomas Williamson titled, *"Dispensationalism and Racism,"* the reader is introduced to the article with the following words *"What would you think of a religious sect that taught that there is one race that is by nature superior, and another race that is by nature inferior? And suppose that this sect taught that the superior race has a divine right to dispossess members of the inferior race and take their properties without compensation, and to ethnically cleanse those who resist this expropriation, using violence if necessary?*[41] Williamson is making the charge that Dispensationalists are racist because they elevate Jewish people to a favored status.

---

[41] http://www.mediamonitors.net/williamson3.html

Actually, much of that quote could easily refer to the Anti-Zionist, however, the absurdity of the above statement is apparent. Dispensationalism does *not* teach that one race is superior to the other. That is like saying that an actual *apostle* of Jesus Christ is superior to those of us who are *not* apostles. It appears the common mistake with these types of claims, is that the people making them consistently fail to understand the difference between *responsibility* and *superiority*. The nation of Israel has been given greater *responsibility*. They are *not* superior to anyone, and normal Dispensationalism does not teach that they are superior.

Greater Responsibility ≠ Favoritism
Each of the apostles of Jesus Christ had a great deal more *responsibility* than the average individual during Christ's time. In fact, they had greater responsibility than did every other Christian who came after them. Their position in the church is *higher*, but they are absolutely *no* different than you or I. Each apostle needed the exact same salvation that we need today. In fact, it is clear from Scripture that God sees *them* as He sees everyone else. There is *no* favoritism with God. None at all. Yet, it was God, who created the nation of Israel and referred to them as His *peculiar* people; His chosen ones. It appears as though the Anti-Zionist has a problem with God Himself.

It was Jesus Christ, who specifically called each apostle by name to be His follower. These individuals would eventually begin many churches throughout Asia and the world. They had far greater accountability than anyone else who would deign to call themselves an "apostle," as some do today. In fact, so great was their responsibility that their names are inscribed in the walls of the New Jerusalem. My name is not. Yours is not. Yet, God does *not* love *the apostles* more than He loves you or me.

Throughout the book of Acts, *after* Jesus had been rejected by the Jews, and *after* He had been crucified, died, was buried and raised from the dead, and *after* He ascended into heaven, it was Paul, who consistently and constantly offered the gospel *to the Jew first* and then to the Gentile. He *never* wavered from that position; always offering the good news to Jews, wherever he went. So was Paul playing *favorites*? Absolutely not. He was obeying Christ's commands, and he made no apologies for it. Did this mean that the Jews were more loved by Paul and by God? Again, no. It means that the responsibility was to offer the gospel message of salvation to the Jews first.

We also see this in action with Jesus in the gospel of Matthew. Here, a Canaanite woman approaches Him and begs for mercy. Her daughter is severely oppressed by a demon. Jesus first responds that His will is to seek and save the lost of the house of Israel. He further comments that it is not right to give to dogs the food meant for the children (in this case, Israel). She then responds with an astounding metaphor of her own, in which she says, *"Yes, Lord, yet even the dogs eat the crumbs that fall from their masters' table,"* (cf. Matthew 15:23-28). Notice that she did *not* disagree with Jesus about her status, or position in life. She understood that it was the nation of Israel, which had been privileged. She merely wanted a few crumbs and her faith was rewarded by Jesus. Jesus' responsibility was to ensure that the Jewish people knew of the salvation that was being offered to them. This was based solely on the fact of the tremendous responsibility given to the nation. Paul continues this throughout the book of Acts. Wherever he went, he offered the gospel to the Jew first, and then to the Gentile.

When Peter gave his sermon on the Day of Pentecost in Acts 2, we see that he is speaking to Jews, offering them the chance to repent and receive salvation. We see this again in chapter three of Acts, and again in chapter thirteen of Acts. He did not see them as people who were *special*. Their depravity was no different from any Gentile's, and their need for a Savior was the same. However, it simply stands to reason that if God created the nation of Israel to begin with, for the purposes of being a light to the world, regardless of anything else, they should be the first ones to be offered salvation.

Williamson continues by stating *"it must be admitted that the modern dispensational movement produces a lot of rhetoric and propaganda against the Arab peoples that can only be described as racist."*[42]

It is extremely interesting that people like Williamson on one hand refer to Christian Zionists as racists, yet, on the other hand, sees no such racism in what *they* believe and espouse. People like Williamson, and the aforementioned Carlson and Valentine, defend the Arab *only*. They are not interested in defending Israel. They are not interested in helping Israel. They are solely interested in ensuring the safety of Palestinian Arabs. How is this mentality free of racism?

An Attack on Arabs?
Williamson refers to a quote by the son of Billy Graham, *"In October, 2000, Evangelist Franklin Graham, son of Billy Graham who has built a reputation for fighting racism, stunned observers with this attack on the Arabs, made during a "Festival" in Lexington, Kentucky: "The Arabs will not be happy until every Jew is dead. They hate the state of Israel. They all hate the Jews. God gave that land to the Jews. The Arabs will never accept that...Dispensationalist followers of the Grahams apparently were undisturbed by this declaration that all Arabs are evil and that they have no civil or property rights in the land of their birth."*[43]

So this is considered an *attack* on Arabs? Although these sentiments have been *openly* stated and *declared* by people like Mahmoud Ahmadinejad, the sixth and current president of Persia (Iran), how are Graham's comments an attack, when he is merely stating *a fact*?

Ahmadinejad is openly critical of Israel and has been for quite some time. His comments are not expressed in secret. He boasts about

---

[42] http://www.mediamonitors.net/williamson3.html
[43] Ibid

them in the open. "*Ahmadinejad's virulently anti-Israel and anti-Semitic rhetoric and Holocaust denial are often matched by other Iranian leaders, and the Iranian regime itself has continued to sponsor anti-Zionism conferences and pseudo-academic lectures and exhibits questioning the fact of the Holocaust.*"[44]

After hearing Ahmadinejad's speech to the U.N. last September, 2008, Abraham H. Foxman, Anti-Defamation League National Director made this statement "*It is clear that Ahmadinejad is deeply infected with anti-Semitism. His statements accusing Jews of dominating and controlling finance and government in the United States and Europe, and of working as a cabal to foment conflict around the world, echo the most infamous passages of the "Protocols of the Elders of Zion." These ideas are classic anti-Semitism by any measure, and President Ahmadinejad has put it on full display for the entire world to see.*"[45]

More Racist Quotes

"*The Jewish nation, it is known, from the dawn of history, from the time Allah created them, lives by scheme and deceit.*" —PA Communications Minister, Imud Falouji, Palestinian television, August 8, 2002

"*We know that the Jews have manipulated the Sept. 11 incidents and turned American public opinion against Arabs and Muslims. . . . We still ask ourselves: Who has benefited from Sept. 11 attacks? I think they (the Jews) were the protagonists of such attacks.*" —Saudi Interior Minister Prince Nayef in Assyasah (Kuwait)

"*They succeeded in gaining control in most of the [world's] most powerful states, and they—a tiny community—became a world power. But 1.3 billion Muslims must not be defeated by a few million Jews. A way must be found. . . . The Europeans killed six million Jews out of 12 million, but today the Jews are in control of the world via their proxies. They lead others to fight and die for them. . . . If we are weak, no one

---

[44] http://www.adl.org/main_International_Affairs/ahmadinejad_words.htm
[45] http://www.adl.org/PresRele/ASInt_13/5361_13.htm

will support us. The Israelis respect only the strong, and we must therefore all unite." — **Malaysian Prime Minister Mahatir Mohammad** (at the opening of the Organization of Islamic States summit October 16, 2003, translation from Saudi magazine 'Ain-Al- Yaqin, November 29, 2002)

"O God, strengthen Islam and Muslims, humiliate infidelity and infidels. O God, destroy your enemies, the Jewish and crusader enemies of Islam." — **Shaykh Jamal Shakir** (Sermon from King Abdallah mosque in Amman Amman Jordan Television Channel 1 in Arabic, March 5, 2004)

"The Prophet said: the Jews will hide behind the rock and tree, and the rock and tree will say: oh servant of Allah, oh Muslim this is a Jew behind me, come and kill him! Why is there this malice? Because there are none who love the Jews on the face of the earth: not man, not rock, and not tree; everything hates them. They destroy everything, they destroy the trees and destroy the houses. Everything wants vengeance on the Jews, on these pigs on the face of the earth, and the day of our victory, Allah willing, will come." — **Shaykh Ibrahim Mudayris** (Palestine Authority TV September 10, 2004)

"The Zionist attempts to transmit dangerous diseases like AIDS through exports to Arab countries." — **Al-Manar** (Hizballah TV, November 23, 2004)

"The Jews are the cancer spreading all over the world . . . the Jews are a virus like AIDS hitting humankind . . . Jews are responsible for all wars and conflicts. . . ." — Sermon by **Sheik Ibrahim Mudeiris** (Palestine Authority TV, May 13, 2005)

"The Talmud says that if a Jew does not drink every year the blood of a non-Jewish man, he will be damned for eternity." — **Saudi Arabian delegate Marouf al- Dawalibi** (before the UN Human Rights Commission conference on religious tolerance, December 5, 1984)

"We will continue our martyrdom operations inside Israel until all our lands are liberated, by God's will. . . . We won't lay down our weapons as long as Jerusalem and the West Bank are under occupation." — **Muhamemd Hijazi** (commander of a Fatah, affiliated militias in the Gaza Strip, Jerusalem Post, September 12, 2005)

Statistical records indicate that from the year 1994 to 2007, a total of 542 innocent Israelis were killed by either suicide bombers, or other bombings. This does not include the number of soldiers killed, nor the number of civilians injured. The perpetrators of these bombings were either from Hamas, or The Popular Front for the Liberation of Palestine, a radical PLO faction, or the Islamic Jihad. These are the types of groups and people that the Anti-Zionist supports and wants the rest of the world to support and respect as well.[46]

These are just some of the people that the Anti-Zionists seek to help; the people who purpose to destroy Israel and the Jews. They have openly declared war on the Jews and on the state of Israel. These people will not rest until every last Jew has been ousted from the Middle East. Yet, because Graham apparently had the temerity to make *factual* statements, he is accused of being racist by the Anti-Zionists. This makes absolutely no sense.

There is something drastically wrong with groups of people who stand for *one ethnicity only*, completely ignoring any and all acts of violence against everyone else, yet have the audacity to call *others* racist. How is *that* position Christian? How are all the teachings of Christ, which we find in Matthew 5 and elsewhere being followed by the Anti-Zionist in these situations?

---

[46] http://www.mfa.gov.il/MFA/Terrorism-%20Obstacle%20to%20Peace/Palestinian%20terror%20since%202000/Suicide%20and%20Other%20Bombing%20Attacks%20in%20Israel%20Since

Don't State That Anything Is "Wrong"
This has been happening in other sectors of society as well. Stand on the street corner and *calmly* make this statement "*Homosexuality is wrong.*" Make sure people hear you, then wait for their reaction. I have made that statement and was told, in no uncertain terms, that my *hatred* and gender bias had no place in a civilized society. I stated it calmly as a biblical fact, and not even on a street corner. It was in the context of a discussion regarding the issue of homosexual marriages. They reacted with name-calling, attempting to deflect the truth by making me appear to be a *hatemonger*.

Yet, if someone says, "Prostitution is wrong," he is not usually met with the same type of rancor. Most will agree that prostitution *is* wrong. We even have laws against it. The person who makes the statement "prostitution is wrong" and does so calmly, without an inkling of condemnation is not looked upon as hate-filled. He is merely making a statement that everyone knows is a fact. Society has long ago determined that prostitution is wrong.

Even though the same set of facts are in place in determining that homosexuality is wrong, a statement indicating it is wrong is met with all manner of retributive responses. Apparently, many within the Gay and Lesbian community believe that if you *accuse* the speaker of being filled with *hatred* and *gender bias* when making such a statement of fact, they will be embarrassed into silence.

Franklin Graham presented a *factual* statement about how the leaders of most Arab countries surrounding Israel, view Israel. Their views are no secret, except possibly to those in the Anti-Zionist community. Most Arabs who agree with people like Ahmadinejad are proud of the fact that they believe as they do. The Anti-Zionist is never seen or heard taking *them* to task for their openly racist comments. The only people the Anti-Zionists take to task are those who stand *for* Israel and the Jews. Incredibly, the Anti-Zionists are not aware of their own racism and hatred. However, they continue to store up hatred for those who believe that God still has an unfulfilled plan for Israel. I can only wonder how they will feel when they learn that Christian Zionism is the correct view, and they end up being desperately wrong.

That Good Ol' Double Standard at Work
The double standard is painfully obvious to all but Anti-Zionists. They reek of self-centeredness, all in the name of God. They resist everyone who is not one of their own, based on their faulty views of the Bible and the promises given to Abraham.

The question remains, were the promises given to Abraham conditional or unconditional? When God said that the Israelites would have the Land of Canaan as a possession *forever*, did He mean until the Israelites mess up one last time, or did He mean forever, as in, until the end of time?

Chapter 7
Will Israel Rise Again?

We will need to spend most of this chapter looking at the promises that God gave to Abraham. We will also need to determine the nature of those promises; are they *conditional* or *unconditional*? In other words, when God gave those promises to Abraham, was Abraham part of a covenantal agreement, in which he was required to do something, which would uphold his end of the bargain? If so, then the Anti-Zionist's viewpoint certainly has merit.

If, on the other hand, the promises given to Abraham by God were *unconditional*, meaning nothing was required by Abraham in order for the covenant to stand and to be fulfilled, then the Anti-Zionist has a severe problem. The determination of who is correct – the Anti-Zionist or the Christian Zionist – stands or falls on whether or not God's promises were *conditional* or *unconditional*. It is truly that simple.

The Promises

The very first reference to any promise given to Abraham is found in Genesis 12:1-3. This is not only the first instance of the promises, but it is our second introduction to Abraham (called Abram at this point in the Scriptures). In chapter eleven of Genesis, his name is introduced to us. Let's see what the text says, shall we?

"Now the LORD said to Abram, 'Go forth from your country, and from your relatives and from your father's house, to the land which I will show you; And I will make you a great nation, and I will bless you, and make your name great; And so you shall be a blessing; And I will bless those who bless you, and the one who curses you I will curse and in you all the families of the earth will be blessed.'" (NASB)

Here, God comes directly to Abram and tells him a number of things:

1. *Go to the land that He will show Abraham*
2. *God will make Abraham a great nation*
3. *God will bless Abraham*
4. *God will make Abraham's name great*
5. *Abraham will be a blessing*
6. *God will bless those who bless Abraham*
7. *God will curse those who curse Abraham*
8. *In (or through) Abraham all the families of the earth will be blessed*

It all seems straightforward. Nothing appears to be hidden, or cryptic. We are not talking about the writings of Nostradamus here. God's desire is that His Word should be *plainly* understood, and that it should be *consistent* throughout. There does not seem to be any coded language here. God is making statements, of "*I will*" to Abram. There appears to be nothing that Abram needed to do in order for God to keep His bargain with Abram. Oh wait! The very first sentence says "*Go forth from your country...*"

People argue that this part of the first sentence makes this a conditional covenant. In other words, God said, "go" and as long as Abram went, things would be fine. If he failed to "go" then the agreement was off. Well, even if we agree (which we do not), that this directive telling Abram to "go" makes this a conditional covenant, it is clear from the following verses that Abram *did* go. The very next verse states "*So Abram went forth as the LORD had spoken to him,*" (Genesis 12:4; NASB). Okay, done. Abram went. Bargain kept. Covenant upheld. Now God is free to fulfill all that He said He would fulfill.

Here is some interesting information to consider, "*Why does the Torah mention all of the great rewards to Abram? Are they listed one by one in order to motivate Abram to respond in a positive way? No, these words do not serve as an enticement so that Abram will go. Abram will go because G-d said 'to go',*"[47]

Did God tell Abram to go, and since he *did* go, this now allows God to fulfill all eight items listed above? However, if we look closely at the verbiage here, God is *not* saying, "Abram, *IF* you will do this and then do this other thing, and keep my commandments, I will do these eight things in and through you." He says nothing of the kind. God is *commanding* Abram to "go," much like a parent would say "*Son, mow the lawn today.*" Please do not try to tell me that the parent is entering into a conditional covenant with his son. A covenant does not even enter the picture. The parent – who clearly has authority over the child – is giving a command and that parent expects the child to obey the command.

---

[47] Rabbi Yaakov Youlus, *Understanding the Language of G-D* (Jerusalem 2003) ,34

This is what God is doing with Abram. He is telling Abram what to do. He is not saying "if" anywhere in the text. This is not a conditional covenant. It is all on God. It starts with God and it ends with God.

Let's say a father says to his son, "*Son, mow the lawn today. After you mow the lawn, we will go to the sports store and get you a new pair of running shoes. This should make running track easier for you.*" Is this a covenant? Notice the verbiage. The parent is *not* saying "if" you do this, I will do this. The parent is giving a command and *when* the son follows through on that command the next thing in line can occur, which in this case is a trip to the sports store for new running shoes. The parent is merely stating the *order of events*. It is a foregone conclusion because he knows that the son *will* carry through and mow the lawn. In the same way, God chose Abram because He already knew that Abram would *comply* by obeying.

Genesis 12:7
Moving a bit further into the chapter, we read these words "*The LORD appeared to Abram and said, "To your descendants I will give this land 'So he built an altar there to the LORD who had appeared to him,'*" (Genesis 12:7; NASB).

We know that Abram had obeyed God because the text states that. As he traveled, he eventually came to the area called Shechem. The text also tells us that people called Canaanites already lived in that area (cf. v. 6). It was at this point that God literally appeared to Abram and made the statement to him in verse seven. What was Abram's response? He built an altar to the Lord there. This was done as a form of worship. Notice that Abram says *nothing*. He is simply on the receiving end of the Lord's statement. God tells Abram to go to a land that He will show him. Abram begins moving and when he gets to that area, God appears and says, "*This is the land I was talking about. This is the land that I will give to your descendents.*" So far, Abram has *done nothing* to earn anything. He has done nothing that would indicate that he was required to do anything to uphold his end of any bargain. As stated, if we argue that Abram was required to "go" then it is obvious that he did go. If that was the requirement, then he fulfilled it. There was absolutely nothing else he was required to do. Nothing. By all counts, God was the only party with any requirements at all in this unconditional covenant. Please note, that God placed those requirements on *Himself*.

Genesis 15

The next event in the continuing saga of Abram's dealings with God, is found in chapter fifteen of Genesis. Here God again confirms His covenant with Abram. As we read chapter fifteen, we see nothing that even remotely appears to be a conditional covenant.

Chapter fifteen of Genesis is an extremely interesting chapter. The reader would do well to take the time right now to read it a few times before moving on. Here, God comes to Abram, again pointing out aspects of the covenant He is making with Abram.

In the previous chapter – fourteen – Abram has just returned from victoriously rescuing his nephew Lot. As he was returning, Abram met the King of Salem, named Melchizedek, of whom the text states he was "*a priest of God Most High*," (Genesis 14:18; NASB). This was an extremely unusual office for a king. As a rule, a person was either a king, or a priest, but not both. Interestingly enough, God had not even instituted the priestly line yet for Israel. King Melchizedek blessed Abram and then Abram did something equally unusual, by giving Melchizedek a tithe (cf. 14:20).

Many commentators believe that Melchizedek is a type of Christ, and there are many good reasons to accept this rationale. Certainly, it is understood that Melchizedek, as priest, presents bread and wine, which remind us of the last supper of Christ with His apostles, as He instituted this sacrament just prior to His crucifixion.

The writer of Hebrews also refers to the "order of Melchizedek" as being royal and unending (cf. Hebrews 6:20). This of course compares with Christ's unending High Priesthood on behalf of all believers.

Later in chapter fifteen, after God Himself has promised Abram an heir, He takes Abram outside and shows him the heavens. God states, *"'Now look toward the heavens, and count the stars, if you are able to count them.'" And He said to him, 'So shall your descendants be,'"* (Genesis 15:5; NASB). God is making a promise to Abram that his descendents will be so vast, they will not be able to be numbered. Considering the fact that Abram was at this point without an heir, this is certainly saying a great deal.

A few verses later, God recounts to Abram what He has already done with and for him when He states *"I am the LORD who brought you out of Ur of the Chaldeans, to give you this land to possess it,"* (Genesis 15:7; NASB). Please do not miss what God is saying. He is crediting *Himself* with taking Abram out of Ur. He gives no credit to Abram at all. So much for a conditional covenant. God is fully in command here, leaving nothing to chance. God took Abram out of Ur and He *will* get him to the land that his descendents *will* possess. It is all in God's hands. No responsibility for any of it rests upon Abram at all. By the same token, this is exactly what God in Christ does for each and every person who becomes a Christian.

The next verse is an extremely important verse, making a very solid point, which should not be missed or glossed over. It says, *"Then he believed in the LORD; and He reckoned it to him as righteousness,"* (Genesis 15:6; NASB). Abram *believed* the Lord and at that moment, God *reckoned* or *applied to his account* God's righteousness. It was at that moment that Abram received salvation! It is the exact same salvation that I received, and you receive (if you are a Christian), and every other Christian receives. It is the salvation that is based on faith and when that faith is evidenced, God then *imputes* to us Christ's righteousness, removing our *unrighteousness* forever.

Allen P. Ross comments, *"Central to the entire chapter is the report of Abram's belief in the Lord and the Lord's crediting him with righteousness (v. 6). This statement is the chapter's explanation of Abram's obedience and the solution for Abram's tensions. Abram received the specific word from God as well as the solemn guarantee that his seed would inherit the land; but the fulfillment of those promises seemed to lag far behind – he had no son, and then he learned that there would be a longer delay when his descendants would be oppressed for four hundred years in a foreign land. It would take faith to wait for the promises; but faith was what God was looking for, and faith made Abraham acceptable to God."*[48]

It is clear then that it was Abram's *faith*, which allowed God to grant him *salvation*. It was nothing that Abram did to secure it on his own. It was faith alone.

Abram's New Birth
From that point onward, God sees Christ's righteousness when He looks at us. He no longer sees our unrighteousness. One might ask how God can do this since Christ had not yet died on Calvary's cross. Very simply, God merely looked "forward" (from man's perspective) to that point when Christ will die, and "borrows" (if you will), or credits Christ's righteousness to Abram's account.

The cross of Christ is always before God, since God exists outside of our time dimension. He sees all of time, all at once. Whether a man lives before the cross, or after has no bearing on the situation. From God's perspective, it is always an *accomplished event,* and as such, the righteousness of Christ already existed for imputation.

---

[48] Allen P. Ross *Creation & Blessing* (Grand Rapids Baker Academic 1998), 305

The Old Testament saint was always saved the same way anyone is saved *today*; through the shed blood of Christ on the cross and man's faith in that finished work. It was never *grace plus works* in the Old Testament vs. *grace alone* in the New Testament. It is *all* grace alone. The good works that anyone does (whether from the Old Testament, the New Testament, or today), all *stem* from the new life that comes into fruition once salvation is received. Those good works are *not* done to earn salvation. They are there as a *proof* that the new life exists within the individual. James makes this clear, as do John and Paul and other writers of the New Testament epistles.

Of course, Abram's next question is a logical one. He wants to know how all of this will be, since he does not even have an heir. How will he be able to *possess* the land that God has promised to him with no visible descendents? The Lord's answer comes in the form of another command in verses nine through seventeen of chapter fifteen.

"9-[God] said to him, "Bring me a heifer three years old, a female goat three years old, a ram three years old, a turtledove, and a young pigeon." 10-And he brought him all these, cut them in half, and laid each half over against the other. But he did not cut the birds in half. 11-And when birds of prey came down on the carcasses, Abram drove them away.

"12-As the sun was going down, a deep sleep fell on Abram. And behold, dreadful and great darkness fell upon him. 13-Then the LORD said to Abram, 'Know for certain that your offspring will be sojourners in a land that is not theirs and will be servants there, and they will be afflicted for four hundred years. 14-But I will bring judgment on the nation that they serve, and afterward they shall come out with great possessions. 15-As for yourself, you shall go to your fathers in peace; you shall be buried in a good old age. 16-And they shall come back here in the fourth generation, for the iniquity of the Amorites is not yet complete.'

"17-When the sun had gone down and it was dark, behold, a smoking fire pot and a flaming torch passed between these pieces. 18-On that day the LORD made a covenant with Abram, saying, "To your offspring I give this land, from the river of Egypt to the great river, the river Euphrates, 19-the land of the Kenites, the Kenizzites, the Kadmonites, 20-the Hittites, the Perizzites, the Rephaim, 21-the Amorites, the Canaanites, the Girgashites and the Jebusites."

There are some extremely important things happening in the text above, and we need to focus on them. The verse numbering has been left in, in order for the reader to locate the verse easier. As we shine the light on this passage, we will have a better picture of the exact nature of the covenant God is making with Abram.

The promises contained in Genesis 15:5 are equally important and the verification of them is the impetus for what occurs next. God is reminding Abram of the original promise; the one we read in Genesis 12:1-3. Beyond this though, God is providing more insight to Abram about these promises, and He will do something here, which serves to ease Abram's mind completely. To Abram though, it does not seem as though God is helping him understand just exactly how this was all to occur since he had no progeny.

Some commentators point out that these promises God made to Abram were not for *this earth* but actually for the next life. This view turns God's literal promises into allegories, which take on a meaning that is not there in the text. Certainly, on one hand, if the fulfillment of these promises was only for the *afterlife*, then Abram had absolutely no reason to worry. Nevertheless, Abram was concerned and it caused tension for him, which he hoped God would dispel.

In response to whether the promises of God were for this life or the next one, R' Moshe Ben Nachman (also known as Rambam or Nachmanides), comments on this. He states *"Now, it never entered [Abraham's] mind that this promise of great reward will be in the World to*

Come, (1) for this does not require a promise, for every person who serves God will find' [eternal] life before Him. In this world, however, there are religious people to whom there befalls [recompense] like the deeds of the wicked; therefore, one requires an assurance. (2) Furthermore, God's warning [your reward is] very great – implied that he would merit to eat at two tables, with all the material goodness that befits completely the righteous people, with no punishment for sins at all. (3) Furthermore, [God's] assurance was a response in kind to what [Abraham] feared. After Abraham made this request, [God] repeated and explained His promise to [Abraham], that he need not fear this childlessness either, for He will make his offspring as numerous as the stars of the heavens (v. 5)."[49]

Beginning in verse nine of chapter fifteen, we read God's instructions to Abram. He is told to bring a heifer, a female goat and a ram, all being three years-old. God also tells him to bring a turtledove and a pigeon. Abram obtains these requested animals and then each of them (except the birds) in half. He then laid each half over against the other.

Apparently, after this Abram simply waited because the text tells us that birds of prey came to try to eat the dead animals, but Abram drove them away. It appears as though Abram was waiting for the sun to go down (v. 12). As it began to grow dark, out of the blue, a deep sleep falls upon Abram.

While Abram slept, a terrible, palpable darkness came upon Abram. At this point, God speaks and tells Abram:

- *His offspring will live in a land that is not theirs, and they will be servants there*
- *His offspring will be afflicted for four hundred years*
- *God will judge the nation they serve*

---

[49] The Torah: With Rambam's Commentary, ArtScroll Series (Mesorah Publications, Ltd 2004), 341-342

- *His offspring will eventually leave with great possessions*

So, God reaffirms the promise to Abram. He also provides more elucidation as well, with details He had not provided before.

Beginning with verse seventeen, the mood of the scene changes. We are told that the sun had gone down, it had become completely dark, and then an extremely interesting and unusual event took place. A smoking fire pot along with a flaming torch passed over the altar and *between* the severed pieces of animals. We then read that God spoke and promised Abram that He (God) will give this land to Abram's offspring. God then outlines the *boundaries* for Abram.

Even though Abram was apparently deep in sleep, God spoke to him in a dream, which was the reason Abram sensed "dreadful and great darkness." So although Abram could not *physically* participate in the ceremony, he could "watch" it from deep within sleep and hear what God was telling him.

We have seen that because the Abrahamic Covenant is *unconditional* in nature, then the promises that God made to Abraham, including the possession of the Land, *will* occur. The only way to get around this, by stating that these are promises to be fulfilled in eternity, is to first of all, say that the Church is the "new" Israel, therefore the promises have been transferred to the Church, and to deny the fact that history reveals that all the judgments from God on the nation of Israel, have, in fact, occurred literally. So, it must be asked, why would only the *judgments* of God toward Israel be literal, while the fulfillment of the *promises* made *to* Abraham, are allegorical?

Chapter 8
Cheerleading for God

Abram slept through the covenantal agreement process highlighted in Genesis 15, because God was showing Abram and everyone else who would eventually read His Word, that this covenant was *unconditional* in nature. It is that simple.

Because Abram was asleep, he could not participate in the process of passing between the severed animals on the altar, which would have involved *both* parties. In doing so, as was the custom, *both* parties would then be agreeing to the terms of the covenant. Unfortunately, very little is known about this custom. However, from the narrative itself (and from Jeremiah

34:18), it is clear that both parties would have walked between the halved and the whole pieces of animals on the altar.

It is this action of walking between the animals on the altar, which provides the contractual agreement of the parties. Since it is absolutely, without doubt evident that God was the only one who in fact participated in the process, only God was binding Himself to the terms of the covenant. Abram's obligations were simply to *receive* what God promised. Does this make sense? Since Abram could *not* be physically involved in agreeing to the terms by walking between the severed animal parts, he had *no* responsibility in the covenant at all, except to *receive* the blessings.

In those days (and even into the days after Israel had become a nation), a covenant was agreed upon and sealed by the process described herein. This was actually the custom of the Chaldeans (cf. Keil and Delitzsch Commentary on the Old Testament, page 137), from which area Abram came (cf. v 7), and in which God chose to use to enter into covenant with Abram.

"The division of the animals probably denoted originally the two parties to the covenant, and the passing of the latter through the pieces laid opposite to one another, their formation into one: a signification to which the other might easily have been attached as a further consequence and explanation...in the case before us the animals represented Abram and his seed, not in the fact of their being slaughtered, as significant of the slaying of that seed, but only in what happened to and in connection with the slaughtered animals: birds of prey attempted to eat them, and when ex-

treme darkness came on, the glory of God passed through them."[50]

We note that in verses 12-17, God has literally placed Abram in a deep sleep as noted by the phrase *"had fallen upon Abram."* This signifies not simply an ordinary sleep, but something that was essentially forced onto Abram. During this sleep, he experienced a prophetic vision. Some commentators believe that the phrase *"behold there fell upon him terror, great darkness"* might also possess a symbolic meaning, in which it foreshadows the future time when Israel will experience *"the departure of the sun of grace, which shone upon Israel, and the commencement of a dark and dreadful period of suffering for his posterity."*[51]

God showed Himself to Abram as a *"a smoking firepot with a flaming torch passed between the animal parts,"* (Genesis 15:17b-18, NET). This is reminiscent of the future when God would stand between Israel and her enemies as a pillar of cloud by day and a pillar of fire by night (cf. Exodus 13:21).

"God alone went through the pieces in a symbolical representation of Himself, and not Abram also. For although a covenant always establishes a reciprocal relation between two individuals, yet in that covenant which God concluded with a man, the man did not stand on equality with God, but God established the relation of fellowship by His promise and His gracious condescension to the man, who was at first purely a recipient, and was only qualified and bound to fulfill the obligations consequent upon

---

[50] C. F. Keil and F. Delitzsch *Commentary on the Old Testament, Volume 1* (Hendrikson Publishers 2006), 137

[51] C. F. Keil and F. Delitzsch *Commentary on the Old Testament, Volume 1* (Hendrikson Publishers 2006), 138

*the covenant by the **reception** of gifts of grace."*[52] (emphasis added)

Ross, commenting on this same passage, states, *"In forming such a covenant, the one who passed through was binding himself by the symbolism, under punishment of death, to fulfill the oath or promise. The holy God would thus be zealous to fulfill his promises, notably concerning the land. He had come down to make this formal covenant, and since he could swear by none greater, he swore by himself. The promises were forever sure."*[53]

This chapter fifteen is a watershed in Abram's life. It is undeniably obvious that God made a covenant with Abram and to his descendants. It is also undeniably clear that Abram had no responsibilities whatsoever.

If this is the case, why then do some believe this covenant was *conditional* in nature? Why is there confusion over the nature of the covenant and the agreement God entered into with Abram?

It is simply because folks who believe this covenant was conditional, base their opinions on what took place *afterwards* with the children of Israel. However, this really has no bearing on God's covenant with Abram, and by extension, to Abram's seed. This is transparent not only from Paul's epistle to the Romans, but also to in the letter to the Hebrews.

The other reason that certain individuals come to believe that God eventually discarded this covenant, is because they believe that the promises are ultimately fulfilled in Christ. The difficulty here is that, while this is true, it is only true in part.

---

[52] Ibid, 139

[53] Allen P. Ross *Creation & Blessing A Guide to the Study and Exposition of Genesis* (Grand Rapids Baker 1998), 313

Paul makes it clear in Galatians that a covenant cannot be added to or changed (cf. Galatians 3:15). However, those who believe that the Church has replaced Israel espouse this very thing that Paul said could not be done!

Jewish men, who had *not* converted to Christianity, saw the early Church as being a sect within Judaism. However, they also noted a lack of obedience to the Law of Moses, as well as a de-emphasis on circumcision (by converts to Christianity; both Jewish and God-fearing[54] Gentile), as an affront to God. This they believed, would in turn, bring judgment on the entire nation of Israel. Since they saw Christianity as a sect within Judaism, they felt that they needed to address the situation and convince these new converts, that circumcision was *still* necessary.

These Jewish men, whom Paul refers to as *Judaizers*, went from church to church, attempting to draw these Jewish and God-fearing Gentile men (now Christians), back into the fold, so to speak. They did not mind if they were part of this new Christian sect (originally referred to as "the Way"; Acts 9:2), but they did not want their involvement in that group to negatively affect the entire nation of Israel.

Their blindness to God's purposes did not allow them to see that the Law, circumcision, and all the rest associated with Moses was simply a *shadow* of what was to come. They could not see past their legalism, which would have allowed them to understand that the Law had been fulfilled in Christ. Christ's sacrificial atonement paved the way for God to grant salvation to people *apart* from the Law of Moses.

---

[54] "God-fearing" is a technical term used by Jews to refer to Gentiles who had abandoned their pagan religion in favor of worshipping Jehovah God. Such a person, while following the ethics of the Old Testament, had not become a full proselyte to Judaism through circumcision (cf. MacArthur Study Bible, NASB, page 1618)

It was this problem, which Paul was addressing. If these new converts to Christianity succumbed to the arguments of the Judaizers, all would be lost. They would, in essence, be abandoning Christianity, and going *back* to Judaism, which was destined to pass away.

Unfortunately, those who read Galatians with a different mindset, understand Paul to be saying that *everything* that God had promised to Abraham *had come to pass*, with fulfillment in the Lord Jesus Christ.

This is not what Paul is teaching. He is *only* dealing with one aspect of the Abrahamic Covenant; that of *salvation* ("in you all the nations of the world will be blessed"). Paul does not touch on any other aspect of the Abrahamic Covenant. He nowhere indicates or implies that the other aspects of the covenant made to Abraham have been fulfilled and/or done away with, and in fact, he verifies by omission, that the other areas of the Abrahamic Covenant have yet to be fulfilled. This he does by not even discussing them, completely leaving them off the table.

Because Paul deals only with the area of salvation in his letter to the churches throughout Galatia, the other essential elements of the covenant (the Land, especially), have not been dealt with by him. Because he has not dealt with the other areas, it is safe to say that they do not come under the banner of salvation, since salvation is the same for the Jew and the Gentile.

The fact that the Land is an issue, which Paul deals with much later in his epistle to the Romans, shows that what he taught and espoused in Galatians, touches on salvation only. This is an important truth, which it appears that many seem to miss.

It seems obvious that if Paul is dealing with the doctrine of salvation *only*, rather than the Land portion of the Abrahamic Covenant, which is not involved here. If Paul is not dealing with the Land portion of the Abrahamic Covenant, then it is yet future. If it is yet future, this is reason enough for the Christian Zionist to support Israel's right to statehood.

In fact, if this is the case, then the Anti-Zionist is not only *far* removed from God's will, by coming against Israel, but they find themselves out on a precipice that is soon to crack and fall away. To be in that position is not only dangerous, but one that finds itself in direct opposition to God's will for Israel. This specific will is separate from the salvation that God provides for Jewish people. The salvation that God provides, as Paul discloses in Galatians and elsewhere, is the exact same for all people; Jews *and* Gentiles. This salvation in no way cancels out other aspects of God's specific will for people and in no way contradicts His *mode* of salvation.

So what we learn from Paul's epistle to the Galatians is that the doctrine of salvation had come under serious attack from those who wanted to add to the finished work of Christ. This then, would involve man's work or effort to gain what was impossible for him to gain through his own strength.

Since Paul is not dealing with the Land part of the covenant, then it can be safely assumed that this aspect of the covenant will yet be fulfilled. This will take place at some future point in time at Jesus' Second Coming to earth, for His one thousand year reign, as He literally and physically will sit on the reestablished throne of David, from Jerusalem.

Chapter 9
Anti-Zionism's Precipice

We have gone over a number of areas with which the Anti-Zionist attempts to affix blame to the Christian Zionist, because of Israel. However, what they merely wind up doing is calling attention to themselves, their absurd opinions, and their hostile demeanor. This is clear from what we have already noted. However, we are not finished. Other Anti-Zionists have much to say not only against Israel, but also against those who support her.

When it comes right down to it, the recurring theme from many websites, books and articles dedicated to Anti-Zionism is found in the one thing in they all have in common: *Anti-Semitism*.

Certainly, no one likes to be told that their views are racist, and this is not a case of getting back at the Anti-Zionist camp by calling them names that may or may not be true. It is pointing out what they *represent*, and what they represent is clearly understood from what they *write* and *say*. Looking at more some examples would be very helpful here and let the readers judge for themselves.

Over the next few chapters (including this one), we will take the time to look closely at specific accusations and jabs the Anti-Zionist uses to attack anyone who disagrees with them. Do the charges they level have any merit whatsoever? The only way to find out is to look at what they say and compare it to *Scripture*. In so doing, we will either wind up proving what they present is truth, or falsehood.

Stephen Sizer's Anti-Zionism
Stephen Sizer's recent book is titled *Christian Zionism: Road-map to Armageddon?* In it, among other things, Sizer attempts to show the history and roots of today's Christian Zionism, and how it became a Socio-Political movement within evangelicalism. Unfortunately, what he winds up doing is producing a book which barely masks his own anti-Semitism.

Sizer is the Vicar Of Christ Church in Surrey, England. His church has an interesting and eclectic mix of associations. Sizer's website boasts the following, "*Christ Church is a member of the South East Gospel Partnership, the **Willow Creek Association** and the Evangelical Alliance* (emphasis added). The Willow Creek Association is connected with Willow Creek Community Church, and Bill Hybels, noted author on church growth, pastors that church.

Anti-Semitism in Evangelical Circles
So before we move any further, even if we were not aware of Sizer by name, or any other writings he has done prior to this most recent book, we know that he is already *against* Christian Zionism. Rick Warren's Saddleback Church is very similar to Willow Creek Com-

munity Church. The emphasis for both churches is reaching out to the one seeking to know Jesus. Because of this, these types of churches are often referred to as "Seeker Friendly" churches.

Every church should reach out to those who need salvation, because salvation only comes from and through Jesus Christ. If the church does not reach out to them, then they are not likely going to hear the gospel message. However, where these churches part company with truly evangelical churches, is that their entire *emphasis* is on reaching out to Seekers, to the exclusion of the need toward Christian maturity of those believers. This is not the biblical model. The church (as we see repeatedly throughout Acts and elsewhere), is to *equip* the saints. If the church is equipping the saints effectively, then those equipped saints can go out into the mission field each week, with renewed strength, faith, and knowledge of Scripture. As they become more and more committed to, and mature in the Lord, their testimony will also become more solid, evidenced by His grace and love. The individual's life then, becomes a witness for Christ, in life, word, and deed.

The church service designed to meet the needs of the existing saint is one in which the Word is *expositionally* preached every week. By expositionally preached, we mean that the pastor goes through the Bible verse-by-verse, in whatever book from which he is preaching. In doing so, the entire context is kept *intact*, and the congregation becomes knowledgeable about the entirety of each book of the Bible, and God's purpose of His inerrant Word for their lives.

Seeking Seekers
Contrast this with a church service for the Seeker. In that service, there is often no pulpit at all. There may be a stool and some type of music stand (if at all), but the focus is not on the expositional preaching of God's Word, but rather the *music* as spiritual "entertainment." The emphasis is on everyday topics that might be applicable to people who are merely trying to "get along" in the world. Salvation,

receiving the Lord, or in their vernacular, becoming a *Christ-follower* is also emphasized. The music is normally very upbeat and in the style of modern rock. Since the music is very upbeat, it becomes impossible to "sit still" and soon, people are standing, clapping hands, swaying from side-to-side, singing along with great fervor, and essentially having a great time! Think rock concert flavor and you will get the sense of the tone here. Essentially, the music is the "worship," not the preaching of the Word of God.

Beyond the musical entertainment, there are usually beverages and snacks prior to the service, so that people can grab a snack before going into the main auditorium. It would not do to worship the Lord on an empty stomach.

Because of all the above, the messages presented are little more than *talks.* We have a number of these types of churches in our area and have attended them. It is not uncommon to hear the pastor speak for roughly twenty minutes at most (usually without notes, or maybe one or two 3 x 5 cards in hand). The message will be interspersed with a lot of jokes, and *possibly* even include a verse or two from Scripture. These verses do not have to be taken from the same area of Scripture because they are only used to emphasize a point.

One such message I heard recently on the radio, was a message about how to have *good friends*. To me, it seems as though these folks are putting the cart before the horse, or maybe they simply have a cart and think they have both.

Christ warns us throughout the gospels that the world hated Him, and because it hated Him, it will hate us. If we are concerned with having and keeping friends, then there is a great chance we are not concerned about the Lord's will in our life. Instead, we are caring about this world, and what it entails. Getting involved in a good, Bible-believing church, where the truth of God's Word is preached consistently, introduces us to other Christians, some of whom we will likely become good friends with. Certainly, being friends with people in whom prayer requests can be shared, as well as the good times of fellowship that are enabled, is worth it, but the gist of God's saving message to man is not about human friendship!

The tragedy of Sizer's (as well as other Seeker Friendly churches), is that they often move within anti-Semitic circles by the company they keep and/or refer to in writing, or in interviews. In one particular interview on Press TV with Alan Hart, Sizer refers in positive terms to American evangelical Dale Crowley, who by all accounts is firmly anti-Semitic.[55] Crowley is noted for his involvement with the Christian Identity movement, which by all accounts is racist and anti-Semitic. Though loosely formed, the people involved with Christian Identity see white supremacy as the objective and lay blame for just about everything on the shoulders of Jewish people. *"The Christian Identity movement is a movement of many extremely conservative Christian churches and religious organizations, extreme right wing political groups and survival groups. Some are independent; others are loosely interconnected. According to Professor Michael Barkun, one of the leading experts in the Christian Identity movement, 'This virulent racist and anti-Semitic theology, which is practiced by over 50,000 people in the United States alone, is prevalent among many right wing extremist groups and has been called the 'glue' of the racist right'."*[56]

Sizer's own opinions and theology have been blamed for causing attacks on Israelis in Israel and Jews in other parts of the world. One such article reads *"...ever since Anglican priest Stephen Sizer launched his crusade against 'Christian Zionists', young Muslim youths are angry at even a church building with the word "Zion" on it, just imagine what it is like to be Jewish in Britain now! Sizer's books Christian Zionism and Zion's Christian Soldiers, his many articles for Muslim journals and*

---

[55] http://www.hurryupharry.org/2009/01/31/stephen-sizer-cites-another-holocaust-denier/
[56] http://www.religioustolerance.org/cr_ident.htm

web sites along with his speaking tours in Iran, Lebanon, Syria, Lybia, Egypt and Indonesia have brought Christian supporters of Israel, whether they are Christian Zionists or not, into the sights of many extreme Jihadists around the world and particularly in Britain. The Spectator magazine, 4th May [sic - should be March] 2009, notes that 'Last weekend the Revd Stephen Sizer, vicar of Christ Church, Virginia Water appeared at an anti- Israel meeting with an Islamist called Ismail Patel. Patel has not only accused Israel of 'genocide' and 'war crimes' but considers Disney to be a Jewish plot and supports Hamas, Iran and Syria'."[57]

Christopher Skinner has written an excellent article detailing Sizer's anti-Semitic leanings. In his article, he states, "*The most disturbing aspect of Sizer's campaigns against Christian Zionism is the association with Islamist ministries. Sizer's article Christian Zionism: A British Perspective was featured in the Friends of Al-Aqsa Magazine, whose stated aim is to "create a momentum with policy makers that will usher in a pluralist society, for Jews, Christians and Muslims alike to enjoy the fruits of this glorious Holy land, as they did during the era of Muslim rule of Al Quds – Insha'Allah"1. The name of this periodical is derived from the Al-Aqsa mosque, which lends its name to suicide bombers. In addition, Sizer was a participant at the Islamic Human Rights Commission conference on 27th February 20032. Is a return of Israel to Islamic rule what Sizer truly desires? Mr. Sizer has chosen some very odd friends.*"[58]

Among other things, Sizer has spoken at any number of conferences, which *oppose* Israeli statehood and presence in the Middle East. Skinner quotes from one such speech by Sizer in which he stated, "Christian Zionists tend to see themselves as defenders of, and apolo-

---

[57] http://barthsnotes.wordpress.com/2009/03/25/moriel-scrubs-article-blaming-stephen-sizer-for-church-attacks/
[58] Christopher Skinner *Stephen Sizer: The Theological Anti-Zionist Crusade* (article located on Scribd.com

gists for, the Jewish people, and in particular, the State of Israel. This support involves opposing those deemed to be critical of, or hostile toward Israel. It is rare therefore to find Christian Zionists who feel a similar solidarity with the Palestinians."[59]

Sizer continues, "*Contemporary British Christian leaders such as Derek Prince, David Pawson, Lance Lambert, Walter Riggans, along with Americans like Jerry Falwell, Pat Robertson, Hal Lindsey, Mike Evans, Charles Dyer and John Walvoord. These writers have a considerable influence in popularising [sic] an apocalyptic premillennial eschatology and Zionist vision on the British Evangelical scene in particular.*

That their teachings warrant the description "Armageddon theology" is evident from the provocative titles of some of their publications. In offering a definition, Louis Hamada traces what he sees as the correlation between Jewish and Christian Zionism.

The term Zionism refers to a political Jewish movement for the establishment of a national homeland in Palestine for the Jews that have been dispersed. On the other hand, a Christian Zionist is a person who is more interested in helping God fulfil [sic] His prophetic plan through the physical and political Israel, rather than helping Him fulfil [sic] His evangelistic plan through the Body of Christ."[60]

Sizer of course, cannot leave Darby and Scofield out of the picture and proceeds to castigate them. In Skinner's article, he continues quoting from Sizer's speech, noting that Sizer states, "*Darby began publishing his prophetic speculations in 1831. Coincidentally both he and Edward Irving began to postulate two stages to Christ's imminent return about the same time. First, there would be an invisible 'appearing' when Christians would meet Christ in the air and be removed from the earth, a process which came to be known as 'the rap-*

---

[59] Christopher Skinner *Stephen Sizer: The Theological Anti-Zionist Crusade* (article located on Scribd.com
[60] Ibid

ture of the saints'. With the restraining presence of the Holy Spirit removed from the world, the Antichrist would arise and the seven year tribulation would begin. His rule would finally be crushed only by the public 'appearing' of Jesus Christ.

There is some speculation that this novel doctrine emerged as a result of the Powerscourt prophetic conference held near Dublin in 1831. 'Darby's prominence at the Powerscourt meetings has led to the supposition that he was responsible for it...' While dispensationalists have been most anxious to perpetuate this belief to ensure a measure of orthodoxy, there is much evidence to the contrary. Several have attributed the notion of a secret, pretribulational Rapture to Edward Irving. Dave MacPherson argues convincingly that the doctrine arose through a prophetic revelation given to Margaret MacDonald, one of Irvings's disciples."[61]

Skinner refuses to accept Sizer's comments as truth, stating, "*Darby's alleged associations with Irving and the origin of his views are fabricated. The key phrase in the above paragraph is "some speculation", which is hardly substantial evidence for an unbiased enquirer but clearly good enough for Sizer. Having read the text of the Margaret MacDonald's prophecy, I can honestly say that there is not a hint of pre-tribulational teaching in it. The sensational titles written by Dave MacPherson (such as The Incredible Cover-Up and The Great Rapture Hoax) reveal a vendetta and should make the reader wary.*

"Darby was not original in his views on the "secret rapture" but he is rightly best known for propagating and systematising (sic) this doctrine. One can find seeds of this doctrine in the writings of earlier Bible teachers such as John Wesley, Matthew Henry and John Gill which Darby had built upon and systematized. John Gills commentary on 1 Thessalonians 4 referred to the coming of the Lord as a "rapture", as did

---

[61] Christopher Skinner *Stephen Sizer: The Theological Anti-Zionist Crusade* (article located on Scribd.com

Matthew Henry. Morgan Edwards was an 18th century writer who believed in a two-stage second coming, a century before Darby. Whether or not Darby was right or wrong is outside the scope of this paper but it should be noted that Darby did not "steal" his ideas from Irving. Dispensationalists, like advocates of other views, argue their viewpoints from the Scriptures and that is what really matters."[62]

So we see Stephen Sizer, with his anti-Semitic theology firmly established by the company he keeps. That is true for all of us. Sizer's church is also part of the Church of England, which is heavily Roman Catholic in viewpoint, especially with respect to the Doctrine of Eschatology (End Times theology). Roman Catholicism has always been more liberal and covenantal in their approach to Scripture. Not viewing any areas of Scripture literally that deal with prophecy, they view most prophecy as allegorical, spiritualizing the passages to mean something else than what is normally stated. As Arnold G. Fruchtenbaum has stated (cf. *Footsteps of the Messiah*), most symbolism used in Scripture is explained either in that passage in which it appears, or in some other portion of Scripture. This eliminates the guesswork completely. Unfortunately, people like Sizer (as well as the Catholic Church in general), seem never to have made that connection, because meaning for prophecy tends to be up for grabs.

Throughout his book, Sizer seems to set out to prove his own theology. It could be argued that all people do this, and certainly, to some degree, that is true. The difference is that those of us who take the Bible literally[63] do so because this is the way language itself is taken; whether spoken or written.

---

[62] Christopher Skinner *Stephen Sizer: The Theological Anti-Zionist Crusade* (article located on Scribd.com

[63] For an in-depth study on how to study the Bible, the author has written another work titled *Interpreting the Bible Literally (Is Not as Confusing as It Sounds)* and is available from his website at http://www.studygrowknow.com

No Difference Between Cults and True Christianity?

Another of the interesting things that Sizer does is that he makes no distinction between *cults* and Christianity. For instance, on page 32 of his book, he opens his paragraph with these words *"Several nineteenth-century Christian leaders in America predicted the imminent end of the world. In 1835, for example, Charles Finney speculated that 'If the church will do all her duty, the Millennium may come in this country in three years.' Joseph Miller narrowed the return of Christ down to 21 March 1843, while Charles Russell more prudently predicted that Christ would set up his spiritual kingdom in the heavenlies in 1914. Russell's success was in part due to the launch of a magazine in 1879, entitled* Zion's Watchtower."[64]

The problems within similar examples of End Times "prophesies" are numerous. Beginning with Finney, we see that his theology was skewed and simply wrong on a number of points, including the error that human beings, who make up the Church, will *actually* prevail in the *hastening* Christ's return, is completely unbiblical. This error unfortunately exists today in certain groups who refer to themselves as Christian. Regrettably, Finney did not see that the times and seasons are clearly in God's hands, and they were predetermined in eternity past. There is *nothing* that anyone can do to delay their coming, or hasten it.

Sizer also includes Charles Russell in this group of "Christian leaders," however, Russell was far from it. He began what has come to be known as the cult of Jehovah's Witnesses. The group was later headed by Joseph Rutherford, who was initially the group's legal counsel. Unfortunately, for the adherents of the Jehovah's Witnesses, there is absolutely nothing Christian about their beliefs. They deny and/or change too many doctrines of the early church. It can certainly be confusing to those who may not know about Jehovah's Witnesses, that Sizer has included them under the label of Christian leaders.

---

[64] Stephen Sizer *Christian Zionism* (England: Inter-Varsity Press 2004), 32

The fact that Sizer considers the likes of Charles Taze Russell to be included as a Christian leader, could very well be that like the rest of his book, with its pointed innuendo, this was simply another attempt at knocking down Christian Zionism. It could also be that Sizer really is *not aware* of the differences between Jehovah's Witnesses and orthodox Christianity.

That aside, what Sizer is hoping to show is that the entire movement to support an Israeli statehood came about because of *man's* doing and not God's. The remainder of that chapter reads like a who's who in Church History. Sizer also never misses the chance to hold Dispensationalism up to ridicule throughout. *"Darby's embryonic and rather rambling dispensational outline, published in 1836, was preceded by a much more developed scheme arising out of the Albury conference of 1830 and published in the Morning Watch in 1831."*[65]

The Anti-Zionist's Broken Record

Complaints about Darby tend to sound like a broken record. Sizer claims that Darby's Dispensationalism began in England in the late 1800s, yet it has been shown that *forms* of Dispensationalism had already been around for centuries prior to Darby. This is also true with the Doctrine of the Rapture.

Even though Darby is unfairly credited with knowledge of Margaret MacDonald's dream or vision of something she called the Rapture, history again shows conclusively that numerous individuals prior to Darby dealt with that doctrine. In fact, there is substantial evidence within the Pseudo-Ephraem document itself, which dates from the A.D 500s, or possibly earlier. Disagreement over Paul's teaching concerning the Rapture abound. However, when taken as a whole, the entirety of Scriptural passages dealing with the Rapture speak for themselves (cf. 1 Thessalonians 4:13-18, 1 Corinthians 15:51-57 and John 14:1-3).

---

[65] Stephen Sizer *Christian Zionism* (England: Inter-Varsity Press 2004), 49

Covenant Theology also has splinter groups prior to being systematized and used by people like Calvin. These are systems that man simply *names*. If their system of interpretation is wrong, their results are certainly also going to be wrong. In the case of Dispensationalism, Darby did not create it. He simply took what others had already been using and systematized it, just as Berkhof took what others were already using and did the same.

Sizer believes that because of the hope of Israel being restored, "*the cause of dispensational Premillennialism [came] to be shaped by Darby and his Brethren colleagues.*"[66] Sizer attempts to make the point that Christian Zionism arose as a political movement out of movements like Dispensationalism, with Darby and others leading the charge. In other words, Sizer more than implies that men like Darby *decided* to believe that Israel would be restored and *then* found passages in Scripture to support his beliefs. Darby et al, then decided to do what they could do, to *make Israel's restoration happen,* which involved propagating and espousing this "false" teaching to as many people as would listen. This is of course absurd, since the views of God's sovereignty held by Darby would preempt involvement in such a travesty. For the Dispensationalist, God's sovereignty is *firmly* intact and of the utmost importance, superseding even salvation. While we believe we are to pray for peace in the Middle East, we know that this peace will *not* come until the return of Christ. There is nothing man can do to bring about lasting peace in that region of the world. Dispensationalists are completely aware of this.

To look *forward* to something is *not* the same as attempting to make it happen. To use an example of this, it would be similar to me looking forward to being with my Lord and Savior one day in heaven. Because of this, I tend to talk about it a good deal. I get together with other people of like mind, and we study the Bible in an attempt to determine what heaven will be like. We think of our loved ones who

---

[66] Stephen Sizer *Christian Zionism* (England: Inter-Varsity Press 2004), 49

have gone on before us. We ruminate over Paul's words to the Corinthians about what our bodies will be like. The thought of heaven is not only inspiring, but because our lives are currently hidden in the Person of Christ, we long for that day.

However, we also balance this with the realization that we are here for a purpose and that purpose overall is to *glorify* God. Witnessing to the lost is one of the major ways to bring Him glory. Living rightly in a wrong world also brings Him glory. So even though we look forward to the time when we will leave this world and our corruptible bodies behind, we understand that God has left us here for a purpose; *His purpose*.

Let us say for the sake of this argument, that suicide is not even an option. As a Christian of course, this fits. I am not allowed to take another human being's life, with the possible exception of defending myself or my family from harm. My reality is that I will be on this earth until the Lord calls me home, at my appointed time. I will go to heaven no sooner, and I will stay here not one second longer. So, no matter how much I look forward to heaven, I am not going there until the Lord calls me home. That is simply the *fact*. However, I can *still* discuss it. I am *still* allowed to be encouraged by what I learn about heaven in His Word. My talking about it, thinking about it, or studying about it does *not* bring me any closer to *heaven*, nor does it bring the moment of my death closer to me. Only the passage of time does that. Knowledge gained simply provides me with a greater understanding of what will ultimately be my heavenly home.

Blame the Christian Zionist
Sizer and other Anti-Zionists routinely blame the Christian Zionist for the tensions in the Middle East. We have apparently brought it into existence by "cheerleading" for Israel, encouraging them to do what they are doing.

The plain fact of the matter is that again, this completely pushes God out of the picture. It abandons and ignores His *sovereignty*. It removes His purposes in the situation. The many passages in the Word, which speak of God's regathering of Israel in *unbelief*, are fulfilled only by God, not by me or by anyone else.

It is *God* who makes these things happen. The Anti-Zionist crowd really gives the Christian Zionist *way* too much credit. If I really possessed the power I am accused of having, I would eliminate abortion on demand, stem cell research, and a host of other immoral practices for which my tax dollars pay daily!

Sizer finally gets down to opening the Bible, comparing it to the beliefs of Christian Zionists and finds the Christian Zionist wanting. This again is no surprise. Sizer has an interesting way of composing his thoughts. For instance, in the opening line of one paragraph he states *"Christian Zionism is constructed upon a **novel** hermeneutic in which all Scriptures are interpreted in an **ultra-literal** sense...this differs from a traditional Protestant or covenant hermeneutic which, while also based on literalism, nevertheless begins with the setting of the author as well as the recipients and is also shaped by the historical, cultural, grammatical and theological contexts."*[67] (emphasis added)

Ultra-Literal? Actually Just *Literal*
Here, Sizer is stating that the hermeneutic used by Christian Zionists is new and built upon something that is man-made. Actually, Sizer has it completely wrong on a number of counts. First of all, the hermeneutic used by normal Dispensationalists (also referred to as Christian Zionists), is *neither* novel, nor *ultra-literal*. These are absurd charges. If I viewed the Bible in an ultra-literal way, then *every* figure of speech would have to be taken exactly *as stated,* not as *meant*. If someone says, "I'm so hungry, I could eat a horse!" then Sizer is charging that I would have every expectation of seeing that

---

[67] Ibid, 108

individual eat an entire horse. The literal hermeneutic *allows* for, and encourages understanding the actual *meaning* of something. In the figure of speech just mentioned, hearing someone use that particular figure of speech would be understood to mean that he was simply very hungry and had chosen an exaggerated way of stating it.

Sizer is absolutely, 100% **incorrect** with his charge that Dispensationalists understand Scripture in an *ultra-literal* sense. Moreover, his statement that the normal Protestant or covenant way of understanding Scripture by using the historical, cultural, grammatical and theological contexts, is equally absurd. While he and other theologians like him, *might* use this hermeneutic with a good portion of Scripture, they do *not* use it when they arrive at *prophetic areas* of Scripture, those related to the end times. For these sections of the Bible, they virtually toss aside the *normal literal* hermeneutic in favor of *allegory*, in which everything is then viewed *figuratively*. In fact, many of these theologians have been heard (or read), making the statement that *all prophecy should be allegorized*. This is simply wrong, as it *covers,* not *uncovers* the true meaning of Scripture.

The Dispensationalist, on the other hand, uses the same hermeneutic - the *Literal-Grammatical* hermeneutic – throughout Scripture. It is this hermeneutic, which considers the *culture* from which the text was written, the *grammar* as used by the writer and its meaning *when* it was penned, as well as the history of that culture and time period. However, as stated, this hermeneutic is utilized *throughout* Scripture, not simply used in non-prophetic passages.

Just Does Not Like Dispensationalism...or Darby
Sizer also again earmarks Darby's Dispensationalism, which to Sizer is *"the assumption that seven dispensations are self-evident in biblical history, if a literal hermeneutic is applied consistently...his actual chronological delineation of these so called dispensations is rambling and*

can only be described as embryonic compared with later attempts to impose a dispensational scheme on Scripture."[68]

We get it, Stephen. You think Darby's Dispensationalism is "embryonic," and "wrong." The truth is though, that Covenant Theologians like Louis Berkhof refer to the various covenants they see throughout the Bible, as being in different *dispensations*. Furthermore, Berkhof, while holding essentially to a Dual Covenantal system (Covenant of Works and Covenant of Grace), lists no less than five various covenants (some of which are minor covenants, or covenants within covenants). Most Covenant Theologians hold to a Dual Covenantal system, while some hold to a third major covenant; the Covenant of Redemption.

Although Sizer has certainly tried his level best (which is not saying much), to shoot holes in Dispensationalism, as being little more than a political movement, all he ends up doing is proving that disagreements seem to be part of the Christian community, and that he does not know what he is talking about. What most concerns God here, in this author's opinion, is how Christians *treat* one another during and within our disagreements. Sizer does nothing to engender a charitable attitude. In fact, what he creates is the exact opposite.

The real tragedy of Sizer's book is that he spends way too much time quoting the vocal minority within Christendom; folks like Hal Lindsey, John Hagee, Pat Robertson, and a few others noted for their sometimes incorrect and even sensational exegesis of Scripture in general. While he does spend time quoting Ryrie, Chafer and Walvoord, he does not spend *enough* time quoting them about the real important aspects of Eschatology, preferring instead to tangle with Lindsey, Hagee and Robertson. The trouble is that none of the latter three mentioned are what might be considered, scholarly theologians

---

[68] Stephen Sizer *Christian Zionism* (England: Inter-Varsity Press 2004), 110-111

(on the level of Ryrie or Walvoord, for instance), though they have written their share of books.

Sizer also continues to quote Scofield's comment related to legal obedience as a requirement for salvation (in his 1909 version of the Scofield Study System Bible). He fails to quote other areas where Scofield elaborated and clarified himself. This continues to perpetuate something that Scofield did not mean. He is accused of teaching that there were/are two methods of salvation; one of grace with works and one of grace alone. Because of this, Sizer and others continually jump on Scofield and Dispensationalists in general. This has resulted in charges of heresy. However, since Dispensationalism does *not* teach two methods of salvation, there is no heresy associated with it. In spite of the absolute clarity of this fact, Sizer prefers to ignore it and continues with his attempts to establish a falsehood as a fact.

However, Covenant Theology, with its two covenants – Works and Grace – without doubt presents *two* methods of salvation. Adam and Eve, according to the Covenant Theologian, were under the Covenant of Works. All they were required to do was *obey* God and *do* what He commanded them to do. Had they done this, they would have passed the test and eternal life would have likely been theirs. As we know, they failed and as a result, flunked out of the Garden of Eden and their perfect environment.

After Adam and Eve's failure, God instituted the Covenant of Grace, we are told by Covenant Theologians. From then *onward*, grace was the establishing characteristic, not works. Salvation was then made available through grace, not obedience. This is clearly teaching *two* methods of salvation, is it not? Unfortunately, what the Covenant Theologian apparently does not realize is that *before* Adam and Eve actually followed through with the *action* of disobeying by *eating* the forbidden fruit, they had already *sinned in their hearts*. It was because they *chose to believe the Serpent*, essentially calling God a *liar*.

It was their *believing the wrong thing* that put them in the position of falling away from God. The actual act of eating the forbidden fruit was simply the *outward* action of what had already taken place inwardly.[69]

The other charge that Sizer brings to the fore that is routinely accepted as fact, is the idea that Dispensationalists avoid evangelizing Jews. He believes that we "*disavow 'missionizing' Jewish people, in part because they believe the Jewish people have a separate covenant relationship with God, which makes belief in Jesus as Saviour (sic) unnecessary or at least not essential until after he returns. Conveniently, it also ensures they receive favoured (sic) status as 'Christian' representatives within the State of Israel.*"[70]

Regrettably, this is simply another fabrication. Individually, Jews do not have favored status. They essentially – as a nation – were given more responsibility by God, because of what He revealed to them and through them. This greater responsibility is often why they seem to be judged so harshly, by God. The Jews of today (as in any day), need Jesus just as much as any Gentile. I know of no one personally who holds to this viewpoint and is a normal Dispensationalist. Sizer's statement is simply untrue. There are numerous organizations dedicated to evangelizing Jewish people.

Scripture clearly indicates that salvation comes only through Jesus Christ. There is no way around that. It is there in Scripture as plain as day. This in *no way* conflicts with any future plans God may have for Israel.

It all boils down to the meaning of *God's will for people*. It seems the Covenant Theologian, or those like Sizer, are forever misunderstand-

---

[69] For a fully study at the issue of Covenant Theology and what Dispensationalism actually teaches with respect to salvation and God's sovereignty, look for the book *His Highest Purpose* at http://www.studygrownknow.com

[70] Stephen Sizer *Christian Zionism* (England: Inter-Varsity Press 2004), 143

ing the concept that while God's salvation for all people is exactly the same, His plan or purpose for people can vary from person to person, but *all* need the exact same salvation; *"For all have sinned and fallen short of the glory of God,"* (Romans 3:23 NET).

God's Plan

What God has planned for *me*, might be far different than what he has planned for *you*. What he planned for *Paul* was quite a bit different from what He had planned for *Peter*. We can fill 1,000 books with comparisons of how God's will is different from one person to the next, and we will have only scratched the surface!

If God has a future plan for Israel (which I believe He does), that plan does not include a *separate form* of salvation. He is not going to *restore Israel* to a place of holiness through their association with Him, *unless* and *until* they first recognize their own sinfulness and need for Jesus Christ. To suggest that the Dispensationalist believes something other than this is to *misunderstand* what Dispensationalism teaches. Sizer proves his ignorance repeatedly in his book.

The implication Sizer continually makes is that Christian Zionism is founded upon error, and has become largely a political party whose efforts, he believes will establish God's rule in this world by *making things happen* where Israel is concerned. This is a fallacy. As stated, no one can make God do *anything at all.* In fact, the Bible is replete with many examples of *God* using people to perform His will even though they were *not* saved.

According to Sizer, the difference between Anti-Zionism and Christian Zionism is the difference between Dispensationalism and Covenant Theology. That Sizer has spent the majority of his book attempting to poke holes in Dispensationalism is clear, as he believes that if he does that successfully, he has also done the same to Christian Zionism, from which he believes it springs. Theologians from both sides have spent time dissecting and vilifying the other's theological system of interpretation. It winds up going nowhere though. Unfortunately, no one seems to win in this debate. Nations and people who bless Israel, will be blessed, according to the promise made to Abram by God in Genesis 12:1-3.

The truth of the matter though is that while Sizer says he has done his homework, it is ultimately merely his opinion, merely cannon fodder. François-René de Chateaubriand is credited with using this term in an anti-Napoleon flyer in which he stated, *"the contempt for the lives of men and for France herself has come to the point of calling the conscripts 'the raw material' and 'the cannon fodder'."*[71] The point is clear. Sizer's arguments do nothing except waste words, with no real effect, except for those who already think as he does. The words serve to distract from the main area of focus.

Does God have a plan for the future of Israel? The answer to this question can *only* be found in the Bible. It is *not* found in opinions or anything that man might define based on his own peculiar predilections. Either God's promises to Abraham were literal and *forever to the end of time,* or they were not. All that is left then is to determine exactly what God's Word says on the subject, not what we *believe* it says based on any presuppositions we may bring to our own personal study of the Bible. Certainly, one of the most important things every Christian can ever do is to determine what *God* is saying in the Word that *He wrote.*

Reading through Sizer's book leaves the deliberate impression that for Sizer at least, Christian Zionism came about solely because of the intentions of *man's* own inclinations. Christian Zionism is a problem to Sizer because of its origins; origins he believes are faulty from the start, due to his poor biblical interpretive methods.

---

[71] http://en.wikipedia.org/wiki/Cannon_fodder

However, in reality, though, Sizer suffers from something that many people suffer from today: *a very low view of God's sovereignty and a very high view of man.* We will deal with God's sovereignty in the last chapter of this book in depth. Before we get there though, we need to look further at more of the charges emanating from the Anti-Zionist League.

Paul Richard Wilkinson, a Christian Zionist says, *"Christian Zionists believe that God is working out uniquely separate, albeit interrelated, purposes with Israel and the Church. This distinction is rooted in the Abrahamic Covenant, which has been described as 'the basis of the entire covenant program,' 'the fountainhead of Bible prophecy,' and 'absolutely pivotal in the entire structure of prophetic truth'...Thus although the Church is comprised of 'Abraham's seed' (Gal. 3:29), it does not fulfill 'the yet unfulfilled provisions of that covenant' which pertain to the nation of Israel, and which the prophets spoke so much about.*[72]

Wilkinson continues, *"Israel thus exists as a nation **outside** the Church, 'with all of God's promises and plans for her remaining in full force'. Christian Zionists make a further important distinction by insisting that the salvation of both the nation and the individual is mediated through the New Covenant in Christ."*[73] This is absolutely biblical. Salvation is the same for Jews and Gentiles. There are no ifs, ands, or buts here. God's promises to Abram remain in full force, even though a few of those promises remain unfulfilled.

The plain fact of the matter is that while many within the Church tend to allegorize all prophecy related to anything even remotely connected to the possibility of a *future* Israel, when it comes to the many times God judged Israel, these are always taken *literally*, at face value. This shows the interpretative façade routinely utilized by Covenant Theologians, who seem more often than not, to pick and

---

[72] Paul Richard Wilkinson *For Zion's Sake* (Colorado Springs: Paternoster 2007), 17
[73] Ibid, 17-18

choose which passage of Scripture they take literally, and which they take figuratively, or allegorically.

However, think for a moment, if the judgments that God is said to have brought upon Israel in the past were *literal*, then why on earth would the *prophecies* regarding the blessings for Israel *not* be taken the same way? Dispensationalism, for all of its opponents, maintains a consistent level of interpretation throughout the Bible, from the first chapter of Genesis, to the last chapter of Revelation.

Metaphors are seen as metaphors with a literal or actual *meaning*, and they are understood that way. Because this is done does not somehow deny that the literal hermeneutic is used. All language, whether written or spoken, makes room for metaphors, similes and other forms of figures of speech. No one is ever expected to take those forms of speech in an *ultra-literal* way, and to do so would be absurd. Yet, when hearing or reading figures of speech and understanding their literal *meaning*, no one is accused of *not* taken the metaphors literally. However, this is exactly what the Dispensationalist is accused of, day in, and day out.

Dispensationalism does *not* employ an *ultra-literal* method of interpretation in Bible study. It employs a hermeneutic referred to as the *literal-grammatical* hermeneutic and in doing so, understands language and the words which make up that language, in their most normal, logical sense.

In other words, the Dispensationalist follows the *sense* of the verbiage. If the context indicates that the words are taken allegorically (as in the case of some idiom, or metaphor), then the Dispensationalist simply looks for the *literal meaning* of that particular figure of speech. This method or hermeneutic is used throughout Scripture consistently without fail.

The Covenant Theologian, on the other hand, *says* that they use this type of hermeneutic, and they do, *until* they get to areas of prophecy. It is at that point, they *stop* using this hermeneutic and begin to look at Scripture *figuratively,* or *allegorically.*

As we have seen, aspects of Covenant Theology (as held by Sizer and others), tend to create a form of anti-Semitism. While these individuals may firmly believe that they are in actuality, being fair to all, they are in truth, condemning Israel, her methods of defense, and often the Jewish people themselves.

Chapter 10

Ugly Words from Anti-Zionists

We all know the little rhyme *"Sticks and stones may break my bones, but names will never hurt me."* The truth surrounding this particular idiom is that adults do not practice what they preach. In fact, while we teach kids that name-calling is wrong, but it should not ruin your day, it only needs to be asked how often name-calling *does* ruin an adult's day!

I spent ten years in the elementary school classroom teaching kids all the core subjects and more. As an elementary school teacher, I was also responsible to ensure that they received so many minutes of physical education instruction per week. Often on top of this, I would have various yard duties to perform, which entailed monitoring the students as they played on the fields. No one wanted the kids to hurt themselves, get in a fight, or climb a tree and jump down, thinking that they would never be able to break a bone.

During those times when students would not be able to play well together, it was usually because someone called the other person a name. They would come running over to me with, "Mr. DeRuvo, she called me a 'witch' with a 'b'!" The other person who was following the first person closely, would vehemently deny the charge. Of course, it then became the responsibility of each person's friends to support their own view of what happened. This made it absolutely impossible to render a verdict.

Normally, in situations like this, the advice that was given was something like "*All right ladies/gentlemen, whoever is calling the other a name needs to stop. Names can only hurt you if you allow them to hurt you. Now please, for the remainder of recess, avoid each other, all right? Thank you.*" Then the students would wander off but would remain within eyesight. As a teacher, when I made statements like the above, I felt like I belonged on an episode of Leave It To Beaver, or some such 1950s TV show. These statements rarely worked, as the verbal combatants would usually stir one another up as soon as the next recess, if they even waited that long.

We teachers would often shake our heads at the nonsense that occurred on the school playground. Come on, these were just *words*. Shake it off. Ignore the other person. Deal with it. Don't be so sensitive. This is what we thought, but we tried to be more constructive with the students themselves because it was obviously important to them. In spite of our efforts, we often felt incapable of providing a permanent solution.

Consider an initial reaction (or desire), when someone cuts anther off in traffic, prompting them to hold up one of their fingers, in a gesture designed to intimidate. Exactly, anger and a strong desire to *do* something back to them. Most of the time, people will respond verbally, or if just as uncouth as the other person, match them hand signal for hand signal; angry word for angry word. This simply stokes the fire. From there, it could easily turn into a major case of road rage, complete with guns, and live bullets. After everything has quieted down, the individuals are left trying to figure out just exactly *why* they did *what* they did. Why did the other person's offensive gesture bother them *that* much? They would give *anything* to relive that day over, assuring themselves they would *not* live it the same way.

So on one hand, when the Anti-Zionist spews verbal toxic waste at the Christian Zionist, there is a part that wants to respond in kind. This of course, serves absolutely no purpose except to heat things up even more. Before it is realized, the world witnesses two "Christians" flailing each other with verbiage like a harvester plowing through a corn field. All of this leaves an interesting taste in the world's mouth. They become convinced that Christianity is worth absolutely nothing. There is the proof, as they knowingly point to the religious debacle before them. Obviously, neither of the two individuals have the 'mind of Christ' or understand the love that He spoke of to those He ministered to.

Is it wrong for Christians to disagree? Of course not. What *is* wrong though is the *way* in which they disagree. It is *the method of disagreement* that often makes or breaks the situation, and brings either glory or dishonor to God.

In looking at some of these other charges, it is important to keep in mind the tone in which they are put forth. The tone or harshness of their words says a great deal.

Another Look at Carol A. Valentine's Anti-Zionism
We will look once again at Carol A. Valentine's comments from the

beginning of this book. Please note that we have separated each individual accusation from her original paragraph, in order to address each aspect of her claims. Her comments are italicized, while ours are not.

Charge #1: Rejecting the Teachings of Jesus?

Fundamentalist Christians" (sometimes called "Fundies") are, characteristically, Zionist, not Christian. In practice, they reject the teaching of Jesus in the New Testament: that each of us is equally precious in the eyes of the Lord.

The accusation that Christian Zionists reject the teachings of Christ is one Anti-Zionists base on *their* perception of what *love* is from Jesus' perspective. Let's look at the definition Valentine uses, which is "*that each of us is equally precious in the eyes of the Lord.*"

What is interesting about this is that no Scripture is used to back up her claims. Certainly, there is a great deal of teaching within the comments of Jesus during His earthly ministry. It might be of interest to know that His ministry extended *only* to "*the lost sheep of Israel,*" (as previously explained). So does this let the Gentile Christian off the hook? Of course not, but like anything else, there is a very specific context surrounding Christ's comments, (cf. Mark 7:28).

While Jesus absolutely *did* teach about loving your neighbor as yourself, and loving people in general, the other side of Jesus that the Anti-Zionist fails to see (even though it is in the very same Bible), is that He spoke more about hell than any other subject. Jesus knew of course that the tragedy of hell exists for everyone who goes into eternity *without* a saving knowledge of Him.

Many liberal-minded Anti-Zionists (like many within Emergent Churches), have a much skewed understanding of just exactly *who* God is, *as* God. While they focus on His love, you will hardly ever hear them discuss other aspects of His character, such as *holiness*, or the fact that He is *just*, or that He absolutely *hates* sin. It is impossible to separate individual aspects of God's character from Himself, yet the leading Anti-Zionists and their followers seem to have no difficulty doing this.

Charge #2: Living in the Old Testament?
Instead, they live in the world of the Old Testament, where a mean-spirited Jehovah played favorites with his children, giving some (now called "Jews") the OK to commit unspeakable acts of barbarism upon the others ("Gentiles"). Read the Book of Joshua if you don't believe this.

This statement seems to say that the Old Testament is not important today because it is in the past. However, she has already made a determination that nearly all prophecy has been fulfilled. Very little remains, she would say. Certainly, there is nothing left for Israel as a nation.

Since the Old Testament is about the past, it is not relevant today for current or future Israel. Beyond this, notice her own opinion of the *"mean-spirited Jehovah,"* whom she apparently sees in the Old Testament. She is admitting that she has absolutely *no* clue at all why God would be justified in ordering the Israelites to completely obliterate the people who were then currently living in Canaan. This is evidence enough of her biblical illiteracy regarding God's purposes and sovereign plans. She prefers rank sentimentality to the truth of Scripture apparently.

God has used the Israelites throughout history to be His arm of judgment, as well as a light to the world. However, as we know, they were extremely inconsistent. God is *not,* nor has He ever been *mean-spirited*. Certainly, His ways are not our ways and the lack of understanding evidenced by Valentine becomes obvious with her own comments.

Charge #3: Living for the Jew?
Zionist Fundies will do anything for Israel and "the Jews," whom they worship as God or God's little brother. They are only too happy to be the Jews' slaves, and insist we all join in their bondage.

This is another falsehood born of complete exaggeration and misunderstanding regarding God's Word. Christian Zionists do *not* worship Jews, nor do they want to become their slaves. Christian Zionists support what they believe is God's plan for Israel. In essence, we are cheering not for Israel to wipe out the poor, unsuspecting Palestinian, but for God's will to come about.

Charge #4: Anti-Christian?
Certainly their beliefs are anti-Christian.

It is easy to make this charge as many do, with each person deciding what the definition of "anti-Christian" means. The Christian Zionist is accused of being anti-Christian because of their *alleged* discrimination against Palestinians. At the same time, what needs to be understood is that if God has an *unfulfilled* will that is *yet* to be fulfilled for Israel, then not only are Anti-Zionists *incorrect*, but those they support are incorrect. In essence, they stand *against* God and His plan for Israel. The Christian Zionist, on the other hand, stands *with* God and Israel. Since Palestinians have deliberately become enemies of Israel, they unfortunately, have become enemies of God, if we are to take the Abrahamic Covenant of Genesis 12:1-3 literally. In it, God promises to bless those who bless [Israel], and curse those who curse [Israel]. When was this rescinded?

The question must be asked, *what is a Christian?* Is it that all men are lost and in need of salvation? Then the fact that both Jews and Gentiles need to be saved, is a foregone conclusion. While the Christian Zionist supports Israel's statehood, their need for salvation also needs to be supported. While the Christian Zionist stands against the Palestinians and anti-Semitism that marks those who oppose Israel, their need for salvation also must be supported. It is not merely a political campaign. At the very heart of the matter is *salvation* for *all*; Jew and Gentile (including Palestinian).

Charge #5: Traitors to America?
More to the point: Zionist "Christians" are **traitors to America***. Along with Jews, they wave the American flag, urging us to spill the blood of any who stand (sic) in the way of Israeli ambition.*

This assumes that Christian Zionists do not pay taxes, support the Constitution, or fight in the military, or any of the other things that have made this country what it is, as a nation.

Charge #6: Screaming for Arab Blood?
Along with Jews, Zionist Christians scream loudest for Arab blood, even though all rational analysis shouts that Israel and Israeli agents in America were responsible for 9-11. Along with Jews, Zionist Christians would happily have America spill its own blood to help Israel realize its ambitions."

One can only wonder how it is determined that Christian Zionists scream loudest when it comes to Arab blood. Her comment "*all rational analysis shouts that Israel and Israeli agents in America were responsible for 9-11,*" is interesting, to say the least. All the theories regarding 9/11 are just that; *theories*. There has been no irrefutable evidence presented, which even *remotely* associates Jews or anyone else, other than the apparent actual individuals involved in the incident, with the tragedies of 9/11.

The Anti-Zionist's Double Standard
What is simply difficult to understand is the fact that no one in the world seems to have a problem with other countries becoming their own sovereign state, except where *Israel* is concerned. Some might grumble, as in the case of Russia's attempted takeover of the nation of Georgia, in 2008. However, the amount of complaining quickly

dies down and, even if the situation still exists to some degree, most forget it and move onto something else entirely.

As far as Israel and the Jews are concerned, Anti-Zionists are resolute in believing that in no way and under no circumstances should Israel *be allowed* to have her own state. Think about this for a moment. Because Israel rejected Jesus Christ, which resulted in His death (which incidentally was the very thing that made *salvation available*), the world essentially says *"Hey Israel! You blew it big time! You rejected the Messiah! You ruined everything! You rejected **God** and because of that, **God** has rejected You! You no longer can become a nation, and you certainly do not have any right to any land in the Middle East!"* Many of these individuals do not even *believe* in God to begin with, yet they still line up against Israel.

Does anyone else see the absurdity in that? No one else uses *religion* to keep another culture from becoming their own sovereign state. In fact, Anti-Zionists would *love* to see the Palestinians take over Israel, in order that an Arab nation could be founded there.

It does not matter that Israel is *surrounded* with Arab nations, all yearning for Israel's blood. Because the world sees Israel (the Jews) as having rejected God (in Christ), it is believed that they do not deserve another chance. Yet, this is *not* God's view.

Who Does Israel Answer To?
The question though is *not* what the U.N. or some other agency thinks about Israel's statehood. Israel does not answer to the U.N. Many countries have "signed on" with the U.N. because they want to appear politically correct.

Israel does not need the U.N.'s, or the world's affirmative nod about anything. Israel will only answer to God. Anti-Zionists decry the Christian support for Israel. However, the same can be said about them and their support of truly aggressive and godless groups like

Hamas. Does the Anti-Zionist care that Hamas has intentionally used innocent civilians as shields against Israeli rockets? Obviously not. Are they aware that Israelis dropped leaflets into the areas that were targeted in the Gaza Strip, giving time for innocent people to get out, and stay out of harm's way in Israel's conflict with Hamas?

Because of these leaflets, Israel gave up her chance for a sneak attack into these targeted areas. What was more important to Israel was that *innocent* lives would be spared. Wouldn't it be wonderful if this same mentality existed within the ranks of Hamas? They seem *unable* to care. Their hatred of Israel is so deeply entrenched and seething that it does not matter to them if innocent Jewish lives are taken.

Unfortunately, the blinders that Anti-Zionists wear do not allow them to see it that way. Their *hatred* of Israel blinds them, and they want no favors for Israel. They want Israel to have *nothing*, and they, like the Arab enemies Israel fights against, do not believe for a moment that Israel is entitled to, or should have *any* of its own land in the Middle East.

Out of the entire world, *only* Israel is judged under a different standard than all the other countries. The absence of logic in this reasoning speaks for itself, yet the Anti-Zionist trudges onward, perpetuating their hatred for God's chosen nation and His peculiar people.

Chapter 11

Is God Sovereign or Not?

God Promises Abram – Genesis 12, 13, 15, 17

In the end, it all boils down to God's Word and God's sovereignty and how individuals view it. Either His Word promises yet unfulfilled aspects of the Abrahamic Covenant, or it does not. Either God controls all things, or He does not.

The Anti-Zionist would like everyone to believe that Christian Zionists are running the world in collusion with Jews, with the ability to promote Israel to power. If this is true, then God is most certainly *not* sovereign, because people would then be in a position to bring things about in opposition to God's plans and purposes. If human beings can override God's plans, then it makes sense that these human beings are more powerful than the God they worship. While it can be argued, that God may have voluntarily and deliberately placed limits on Himself, when He gave humanity free will, it is never stated or implied in Scripture that human free will is *capable* of standing against God or His purposes.

The crux of the matter lies in each person's view of God, and His sovereign purposes. The vitriol, the anger, the mean-spirited rhetoric, and all the rest that marks the speech and writings of the Anti-Zionist, speaks for itself; at least to those who have the ability to see and understand.

Anti-Zionism's venomous tirades against Christian Zionism, Israel and the Jewish people in general, are evidence enough of their own attempts to thwart God's purposes. Their hatred of the Jewish people is the same hatred that prompted the Inquisitions as well as the Holocaust of Hitler's regime. It is difficult to make these pronouncements, but it is even more difficult *not* to do so.

How anyone can call himself a Christian and hate the very people through which salvation came to the world is something that is born in *hell*. It stems from Satan's own destructive forces he wields against the Jewish people from time immemorial. His hatred of the Jews has never been hidden, though he routinely hides behind those he chooses to do his work for him. Often, these individuals are unaware of his purposes, and his abject hatred. They view Scripture through his twisted reality, in which he hopes to bring a final and complete assault onto God's chosen people. His efforts have been, and will be completely futile. He has never stood against God and never will stand against Him.

Sadly, many of those within the nation of Israel will die without knowledge of Christ and the salvation that is only available through Him. Do the Anti-Zionists care? They do not appear to care, though they believe that their own virtue is firmly intact and their real, underlying motivation is for *all* people. Unfortunately, their words belie their actual motives. They see Jewish people and those who support them as the enemy, not only of God, but also of His purposes.

I am convinced that this situation will only continue to heat up, with more vitriolic rhetoric tossed around like a chef mixing a salad. It stands to reason that this hatred of Jewish people, and the belief that Israel has no right or reason to be involved in the Middle East, will escalate until it will reach a fevered pitch. At that time, things will be perfect for the Antichrist to step onto the world's stage, pretending to have concern for Israel and the Arab situation. He will gain their trust and provide a solution to the problem, which will allow Israel to build at least some aspect of the Tribulation Temple. This in turn, will allow them to begin once again, the sacrificial system. That will allow them to to call upon their God. All of this is outlined carefully in Daniel 9.

In the middle of the last "week" of human history, the Antichrist will pull the plug on his covenant with Israel. He will turn against them as no other dictator has ever done, or will ever do again. The people of Israel will see and understand that they have not only been betrayed, but they have spent generations being *deceived*. From that group, God will call out His Remnant.

This Remnant, at the end of the Great Tribulation, will go in and possess the Land that was promised to Israel, long ago, as recorded in Genesis 12, 13, 15, and 17. Jesus will reign from Jerusalem, and will do so with a rod of iron, which is evidence enough that not all will be in agreement with Him. However, this will not matter, and it will certainly pose no threat to Him or His rule.

For 1,000 years, while Satan is to be chained in the pit, Jesus will reign upon the physical earth, *proving* that He has gained the victory over Satan; proving also that He is the *rightful owner* of this planet. Once the 1,000 years are accomplished, Satan is released and will attempt a final overthrow of Jesus. Utterly failing, Satan will be judged at the Great White throne, along with all the rest of mankind who rejected Christ, going into eternity without His salvation. All of these will be tossed into the Lake of Fire, where they will exist in torment forever.

Following the Great White throne, this earth will be destroyed by God Himself. He will then create a brand new one and once that is accomplished, the future eternal order will begin for all. It is at this point, that the truth of what Paul speaks of in Galatians regarding the distinctions between man and woman, Jew and Gentile, and slave and free will go into effect. In the eternal order, there is no difference, as all will live with God in perfect harmony and without sin, something that no amount of trying could accomplish here on this planet, even during the millennial reign of Christ.

The Anti-Zionist fails to recognize God's future plans, not only for Israel, but ultimately for Himself. Christ *must* reign on the earth, from David's throne, because He promised that He would. To decide arbitrarily that Jesus reigns from His Father's throne in heaven, is really what He meant by saying that He would rule from David's throne, thoroughly misses the point and changes Scripture to mean something it does not mean.

The Anti-Zionist would do well to look at themselves and their demeanor. Hate-filled anger seems to be the hallmark of their objections to Christian Zionism. It is either righteous anger, or unrighteous. It would appear that, from all aspects of Scripture, righteousness is not part of their thinking. They seem devoid of the most basic understanding of God's Word with respect to His sovereignty, and His plans for Israel.

God will bring about the fulfillment of these as-yet unfulfilled aspects of the Abrahamic Covenant for no other purpose than because His Name has been dragged through the mud. It is His Name that He seeks to purify. He will do this by fulfilling the promises He made to Abraham. He will bring all of what He promised to fruition because His Name will be cleared. His Name will no longer be seen as something held up to ridicule. He will be high and lifted up through the fulfillment of all that He promised to Abraham, not only salvation, but the other aspects of this covenant as well.

God is not limited or held back by anyone. The Anti-Zionist has it wrong on many counts. God is fully sovereign and He has never abdicated His heavenly throne to anyone. Though many have tried to overthrow God, none has been successful, nor will anyone ever be successful.

Anti-Zionists must cease their attempted vilification of God and of those who support God and His purposes with Israel. They need to look at themselves and recognize that their anti-Semitism comes from no other source than *Satan* himself.

Christian Zionists look to the future, when all of God's promises will be fulfilled. We do not do this because we worship Jewish people. We do not do this because we wish to be enslaved to them. We look to the fulfillment of God's promises for no other reason than because God has promised it, and He will fulfill it.

May God open the hearts and minds of all who oppose His purposes. He will be glorified. May we stand with Him in praise and adoration as He glorifies Himself. Amen.

NOTES

Order Other Books by Fred DeRuvo

www.createspace.com • www.amazon.com • www.studygrowknow.com

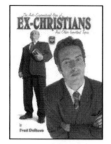

The Anti-Supernatural Bias of Ex-Christians (and Other Important Topics)
Look into the testimonies of folks who refer to themselves as Ex-Christians. Are they, or are they kidding themselves? Fred goes back to the Bible to determine the truth of their words. Other topics deal with the Rapture, the Israelites as slaves in Egypt and more. 240 pages, $14.99, 7 x 10 format

Between Weeks
The 70 weeks of Daniel, highlighted in Daniel 9:24-27 are there for our benefit. God did not *need* to tell us anything, but He chose to do so in order that we would be blessed by the information He has graciously provided to Daniel through the angel Gabriel. 70 pages, $9.99, 7 x 10 format

Christianity Practically Speaking
As a Christian, do you ever feel like it's just not working, where the rubber meets the road? Is it your expectations, the Bible's, or a bit of both? Fred seeks to explain Christianity in practical terms that every Christian can appreciate. 100 pages, $10.99, 7 x 10 format

A Deceptive Orthodoxy: the End Times "Gospel"
Far too many individuals believe the real apostasy-causing problem is found in the PreTrib Rapture. Because of this, these same individuals have precious little time to combat the actual deception that has invaded the visible Church and leaving full blown apostasy in its wake. Unfortunately, lost souls hang in the balance. The Great Commission has never been rescinded. 204 pages, $13.99, 7 x 10 format

Interpreting the Bible Literally (Is Not As Confusing As It Sounds)
Unfortunately, too many Christians today are not aware that in order to study and interpret Scripture, certain tools (or methods) must be applied. It's like learning a foreign language, complete with idioms and other forms of figurative language. 142 pages, $12.99, 7 x 10 format

Resources for Your Library:

BOOKS:

- Basis of the Premillennial Faith, The, by Charles C. Ryrie
- Biblical Hermeneutics, by Milton S. Terry
- Daniel, the Key to Prophetic Revelation by John F. Walvoord
- Dictionary of Premillennial Theology, Mal Couch, Editor
- Daniel, by H. A. Ironside
- Daniel: The Kingdom of the Lord, by Charles Lee Feinberg
- Daniel's Prophecy of the 70 Weeks, by Alva J. McClain
- Exploring the Future, by John Phillips
- Footsteps of the Messiah, by Arnold G. Fruchtenbaum
- For Zion's Sake: Christian Zionism and the Role of John Nelson Darby, by Paul Richard Wilkinson
- Future Israel (Why Christian Anti-Judaism Must Be Challenged), by E. Ray Clendenen, Ed.
- God's Plan for Israel, Steven A. Kreloff
- Israel in the Plan of God, by David Baron
- Israelology, by Arnold G. Fruchtenbaum
- Moody Handbook of Theology, The by Paul Enns
- Most High God (Daniel), by Renald E. Showers
- Mountains of Israel, The, by Norma Archbold
- Pre-Wrath Rapture Answered, The, by Lee W. Brainard
- Prophecy 20/20 by Dr. Chuck Missler
- There Really Is a Difference! by Renald Showers
- Things to Come, by J. Dwight Pentecost
- What on Earth is God Doing? By Renald Showers

Made in the USA
Charleston, SC
18 January 2010